PORSCHE
Owner's
Companion

PORSCHE
Owner's
Companion

*a Manual
of Preservation
& Theft Protection*

Dan Werner Post

POST-ERA BOOKS
Arcadia, CA 91006

Author's Note

While products in popular use are mentioned occasionally by trade name, blanket endorsement is not intended. A concerted effort has been extended to outline procedures believed to produce superior results. Since conditions and applications may vary greatly, however, no guarantee of particular results is expressed or implied. All recommendations are presented as a guide. Final judgment in both product selection and technique rest with the captain-of-the-ship – the owner.

As it appears in this work "Porsche" is used to designate a particular make of automobile. The manual is an independent effort and no affiliation or relationship with the car's builder or its distributors is inferred.

FOREWORD

The car salesman had worked hard to close the deal with his difficult prospect. While Mr. Stone had masqueraded throughout the presentation as a rough-cut sophisticate he had, early on, distinguished himself more clearly as a rather dull tool. In naive abandon he had just waved away without a glance the proposed installment contract offered for his review. The salesman's unflagging courtesy continued as he moved to wrap up the deal.

"Now, Mr. Stone, I'll reconfirm these figures on this calculator and we'll see exactly how little your beautiful new Mercury is going to cost you."

The consumer's reply was sharp and conclusive. "Just tell me *how much* the payments are." Then he finalized in arrogant pretention, *"I don't want to know how many."*

Fortunately, few would try to conceal practical illiteracy with a remark so measured to exhibit the brain as a fiscal wasteland. Most drivers today are literate and responsible. Some may have even discovered owner's manuals in their glove boxes and spent a few moments actually reading them.

For the average motorist that venture into the dash compartment is about the end of the line in getting to know his car. Only wear, tear, or perhaps mischiefmakers or thieves later force an issue that bestows him with further knowledge of his automobile after the fact. The typical operator exercises his driving right to the fullest. No more consideration is given to reading a book that purports to show him how to enjoy owning and operating his Pinto than he would give to a manual telling him how to go to the bathroom alone.

"Porsche automobiles have always set themselves apart from normal means of transport and they will differentiate themselves clearly in the future as well," summarizes Prof. Dr. Ernst Fuhrman, recent chairman at Porsche. "We draw the courage for this endeavor from the attitude of our customers who are not only willing to pay more money, but to invest this money in matters for which the average auto buyer has no use and no understanding."

The Porsche owner *is* someone apart. The very nature of his car makes this so because it was evolved from a different plan. Rare is the case where this *marque* was chosen in a casual draw against other contenders. More often, selection resulted from competent study and a cultivated passion for those attributes that particularly distinguish the Porsche from the field.

Many years ago the editors of *Road & Track* shrewdly offered the following description of a typical Porsche owner. "The word is *serious*. The driver will take himself and his driving seriously. Damned seriously, in fact." So it is that the enthusiast probably became familiar with the saga of Professor Ferdinand Porsche and his cars, by chapter and by verse, before he located his own first car.

When it comes to enjoying the car to its fullest dimension, proper knowledge is the key. "Drive a Porsche and the world is apt to take you for an expert," observed *Automobile Quarterly* in a retrospective.

The Porsche adventure — appreciated among the initiated as *driving in its finest form* — can only be enhanced by effectively preventing deterioration, devaluation and piracy. The **Porsche Owner's Companion** has set its sights on coordinating the legend of supremacy with the special service lore left largely undefined by the prevailing list of operation handbooks. It enumerates in convenient form that considerable body of frequently overlooked facets in ownership that the individual owner might not otherwise fully assimilate even over a period of several years of driving.

Experts in many different Porsche-related fields have been consulted in the compilation of this unique guide. From the insight of the seasoned hobbiest to the sage advice of the professional, the reader has before him the knowledge that will provide a headstart in fostering longevity for the car and extracting maximum pleasure and satisfaction along the way.

A crisp, straightforward text is supported by line illustrations specially drawn by the popular motoring artist Bill Dobson and by photographs chosen largely from the author's own work. Some depictions have been intentionally selected to overstate condition or circumstance for particular emphasis. While the prideful owner who has never permitted his car to get away from him may never witness such gross reality, the restorer, starting out with a *Two* or *Three* point car on the *Ten Scale* will understand.

Ideally, this work is intended to reduce the need for reflection on that time-honored axiom: *If I had only known then what I know now.*

— The Publisher

ACKNOWLEDGEMENTS

A manual of this scope cannot be produced without access to many records, public and private, and without assistance from knowledgeable sources. The author was fortunate in obtaining the support of a number of seasoned specialists whose particular technical guidance substantially advanced this work.

Primary tribute must be expressed to the two Ferdinand Porsches — father and son — whose firm objectives led to the conception and production of this unique automobile. The House of Porsche is also honored for having extended that original ideal to this day by continuously embodying in its cars such a particular aura of charm that virtually every Porsche owner has become a Porsche fan.

A note of gratitude is due John Andrews, the late Peter Gregg, Donald Hage, Phil Hill, Manfred Herrmann, Ronald Irwin, Andreas Koeper, Lael Littke, Richard Mauch, Ken Merfeld, Jim Sitz, Jürgen Strommel and Don Whaley, whose expertise and suggestions were particularly helpful. A word of appreciation is due professionals Bill Dobson and Brian Shepard for their care in specially producing line illustrations.

Acknowledgement is due various American and European periodicals — apart from those listed in the Bibliography — from which details were confirmed. Special thanks to assisting staff members from the Colorado Springs, Colorado and Los Angeles and Pasadena, California, public libraries.

Additional details were developed from reference to the back file of Porsche *Panorama*. Appreciation is especially due Roger W. Chaney, Robert R. Gelles, Hank Malter, Norm Martin, Jim Perrin, Charles Stoddard, Robert A. White and other officers of PCA — past and present — for an unremitting contribution of time and experience in the cause that enthusiasts in the United States might enjoy a club affiliation consistently fitting for the Porsche owner.

Special credit is extended to the Porsche Audi Division of Volkswagen of America, Inc. for permission to reprint statistics from *The Porsche Family Tree*.

Lasting thanks are also expressed to a set of parents whose interest and encouragement were unending.

— Dan W. Post

CONTENTS

INTRODUCTION

The mountain forest was ablaze with the colors of new growth. Sunlight from a spring morning cast long beams of filtered light down through the trees onto the narrow road that wound through a needle packed floor. As he threaded his car through the pass, he reveled in the way its response to his every demand was so instant, *so right*. It reconfirmed the pedigree he had enjoyed anew each time they had been together. *It gave so much and asked so little.*

In that respect the car reminded him of the faultless character of his wonderful *Lisa,* the pure canine product of one hundred years of German Shepherds.

Venerated maturity in engineering . . . timeless simplicity in package design . . . celebrated concern for detail . . . glove-like handling control . . . These are some of the attributes embodied in an automobile that ranks as the *Schäferhund* among sports cars with virtually everyone in the motor world.

Another favorable consideration is *intrinsic worth*. Porsche has demonstrated the capability of remaining an asset over as many years of operation as its owner may elect, rather than becoming a liability with age like the average automobile.

Until some of the largest car makers were shocked recently into taking a second look at themselves and the *real* market, motor manufacturers generally, and the domestic industry particularly, had assembled their wares on a premise of built-in discontent, coupled with the false idea that *bigger was better*. Through continuous shuffling of engineering and cosmetic specs, planned obsolescence had been achieved and a replacement market assured.

Who is the winner in this game?

Not the consumer. Mortality rates reveal that this was a very successful way to be in the business of building and selling automobiles to an *undemanding* public. The median lifespan of the average domestic automobile has been established as about seven and sometimes as much as ten years. Six million cars are scrapped yearly in the U.S. alone.

Who loses out in such an expendable system?

Not the manufacturers. Yesterday's second largest investment for the average individual consumer depreciates predictably in just these few seasons to metal salvage value. The American automobile was once called "the greatest value for money in the history of the world." How quickly the value fades. One owner of a big *Town & Country* wagon, tarnished only in the sense that it ran eight miles to the gallon, recently tried for a deduction by offering his golden chariot to the Salvation Army. Thanks, but no thanks. "If you can't sell it; neither can we," he was told.

Must this anguishing experience continue to be the average owner's fate every few years? Does it have to be?

Now that government edicts govern fuel efficiency for the automobile industry, the die has been cast. For the first time in eighty years of carbuilding, American makers have had to rethink the form their products should take.

Now who will lose?

Vehicles will be progressively reduced in size so that "bigger" will no longer be touted as "better." That's about the only real change that will take place. Any student of American mass-production knows that this will not affect the industry adversely in its own best interests, this offering of a different size product. These cars will continue to be built with commercial considerations coming first. The industry observer knows that the domestic car regardless of its future package size, will still carry all those built-in measures to assure expendability in performance and in styling so that its buyer will be compelled to re-enter the market, at the extreme, only a few seasons after his latest purchase.

Like tires that wear thin and batteries that fail, the average automobile begins to decline from Day One because it was and will continue to be *built for replacement*.

At Porsche a different set of rules has governed the game of car building from the beginning. Recognizing that optimum performance and satisfaction are simply not compatible with change-for-the-sake-of-change, a policy was established confining changes to *refinement of the proven*. Ecologically relevant materials were used where possible. As a consequence, few "all new" models have been introduced to the public since Porsche production began more than three decades ago.

Endurance has been inherently built into what was — at least until recent years — practically a singular blood line. "The difference must be durability, something Porsche has always stood for," confirms Lars Schmidt, a member of Porsche's board of management.

So it would appear that the highly efficient and durable Porsche is a product based on the very antithesis of general motor industry trends in engineering and in marketing.

Who wins under these rules?

Everyone does. Both the manufacturer and the owner. Notice that in this instance the buyer is no longer called a *consumer,* but an *owner.* The builder wins by providing a basis for rendering satisfaction to the buyer. The owner wins because he actually receives what he anticipated when he purchased his car. As time passes, this creates a circular response of mutual respect. It is the difference between building maximum *package* per package and maximum *efficiency* per package.

Internationally, the automobile industry's time-honored concept of "bigger is better" was never really successfully refuted until the arrival of the Porsche on the world scene. Till then the buying public had been thinking that *a smaller car should cost less,* because — all things considered — it is *less* car.

Then came the Porsche. The avant garde was quick to accept "less" car — a smaller package — while paying a premium for the privilege. So it was that from the beginning the Porsche attributes have been self-evident among a certain driving elite.

One of the ablest principals in contemporary American business, Otis Chandler of the Times Mirror publishing empire, can afford any vehicle for any purpose. He has long been recognized for his objective collection of the grand classics — Mercedes, Rolls, Duesenberg and others.

Less known to many is the fact that he has relied upon Porsches as his principal personal transportation for more than fifteen years. Alongside the Turbo he uses daily as this is written, are an array of others, including two 917s.

Queried as to his weakness for these cars in view of his obvious palate for the mighty milestone makes, Mr. Chandler responded solemnly, "I appreciate mechanics and aesthetics in the classic cars. So it follows that I can find the same things to appreciate in a Porsche."

Even as the long-docile, consuming American public began to demonstrate widespread interest in more fuel-efficient cars for general transportation. Detroit was stubbornly reluctant to acknowledge the true merit of optimum engineering and small packaging as a *plus* rather than a *minus*. As recently as 1980, General Motors Corporation Chairman Thomas A. Murphy, when interviewed on CBS *Face the Nation,* declared that small foreign automobiles share "too much of the market," blaming American consumers who buy them for a weakness for the "fashionable."

As this is composed, more than 600,000 auto workers are currently victims of layoffs across the nation. It is apparent that these men and women suffer from a major miscalculation on the part of the industry in failing to conform to a sophisticated public's more practical demands.

Yet, Douglas A. Fraser, president of the United Automobile, Aerospace and Agricultural Implement Workers of America (UAW), persists in attributing the unemployment problems to foreign manufacturers' "eagerness to exploit" the American market. In an interview with *U.S. News & World Report* Mr. Fraser went on to declare that consumer loyalty to foreign cars is resulting in permanent damage to the U.S. auto industry.

From these views, *the crime seems to be one of giving enlightened American consumers what they want and need.*

Refreshing for its honesty is the analysis made by Joseph E. Coberly, Jr., a long-established Ford dealer in downtown Los Angeles. "The American auto companies are suffering because they made bad decisions — produced too many big cars for too long — and because government regulations, the government-caused energy crisis and inflation have taken the starch out of American business."

14

Alas, U.S. manufacturers have begun to take a serious second look at values heretofore unseen. Witness the Chairman of the Ford Motor Company Philip Caldwell's recent discovery. "Luxury doesn't have to be measured in physical size," he observed in a June, 1980, interview in *U.S. News & World Report.* "There are things such as smoothness and ease of operation and quietness to consider. In the future, we won't measure luxury by size alone."

Unfortunately for the general public, Porsche and the balance of the motor industry will continue to move poles apart in their objectives. The driver of the new wave high performance compact, whether it comes from Detroit or from abroad, will remain a *consumer,* while the driver with his Porsche will still be an *owner.*

"As cars become more and more alike in appearance and performance," predicts Helmut Flegl of Porsche's R & D facility at Weissach, "there will always be people looking for something different — and Porsche *is* something different."

Responsibility for sustaining this *difference* has been handed down with reverence from manager to manager. "Cheap little cars without any technical know how," observed long standing board chairman Ernst Fuhrmann, "can be produced in any country." What will continue to distinguish Porsche from the pack was made clear with his further statement that "For us at Porsche the development of the modern super car is the major task of the future."

American *aficionados* could be in for a special treat with the form of cars to come. As this is written, Peter W. Schutz, a German-born American citizen who emigrated as an infant was named to replace Dr. Fuhrmann as CEO at Porsche. His experience with U.S. motoring conditions is first hand. Schutz grew up, learned to ride a scooter, then a bike and later to drive, all in the United States. He returned to his native country only three years ago.

Each individual Porsche represents a particular moment of achievement in the gallant history of the automobile which is its owner's exclusive preserve. An enthusiast is never intimidated by another owner's more recent model. Comraderie among Porsche drivers has become legendary, exerting equal unified force both forward and backward through the production years.

One of the world's greatest living fine arts photographers, Brett Weston, is highly acclaimed for his total control of the medium, unique sense of order in composition and lack of commercialism. Commenting playfully in a candid interview for *American Photographer,* he offered the following, "Money is nice to have, but no disaster not to have. My photography is what I must have." Then after a pause he added, with what was said to be an impish smile, "And I think I should have a Porsche."

Driving a new 928 is naturally a pleasant private and public experience. But so is driving last decade's 911, or one of the 356 models that has already spread joy for a generation.

Witness Anthony Lapine, Porsche's styling chief, who still uses the 1600 Carrera he bought new in 1959 as his personal car. *It is the only Porsche he has ever owned.*

No stigma is associated with using any Porsche . . . *unless it is not being maintained.* Regular driving should be the end product of ownership. The Porsche was built to go and thrives on the run. Nonetheless, Porsche's unique character among automobiles — being publicly regarded as occupying the place in the apex of the automotive pyramid — practically dictates that the owner fulfill an unwritten obligation to society by driving his car only when it is in exemplary form.

A retrospective moment in Ferry Porsche's autobiography, *We at Porsche,* confirms this thought in a tribute to his father. "He [Ferdinand Porsche] was a perfectionist who liked his cars not only to run right but also to *look just like new.*"

1
OWNERSHIP

Driving:
an Adventure in
Perfection

With the factory's departure from a dedication solely to the rear-engine air-cooled concept — in order to engender a front engine, liquid-cooled species alongside the chassis of tradition — the name *Porsche* has assumed a broader meaning. The 928 and 924 are real.

Lower 900 series and 356 cars are no less real. Presently, these earlier Porsches, with the validity of their character distilled by time, are among the most cultivated by the purists — those owners who know and appreciate the scientific simplicity that went into designing a scalpel to be *perfect* for its purpose, or aircraft controls to permit banking and climbing like a bird. To these owners the Porsche represents *perfection in a driving tool*.

Today, with the rear engine concept gradually being reduced in numbers at the production level, these cars assume the status of the *classic,* which Merriam-Webster's *Third International Dictionary* defines as:

"Having recognized and permanent value of the highest rank; of enduring interest and appeal; characterized by simple lines correct for a variety of places and occasions; basically in fashion year after year."

Porsche began construction at the beginning with an underlying challenge as motivation: to build the most efficient and reliable automobile possible, leaving only proper maintenance as the inducement for holding and enhancing those qualities as the car charged into the years of service that would lie ahead of it.

17

Survival in traditional style for any out-of-production model requires protection. The best umbrella for the Porsche is the appreciative, dedicated owner. The critical aspect in owning this classic lies in how the *whole car* is regarded by its present owner. To preserve the Porsche as a capital asset, engine maintenance becomes only one consideration. Body details, trim, *originality,* all must be kept with equal concern. The enthusiast-owner knows that he has a personal stake to protect and that everything done to the car in the future will either tend to sustain and appreciate value or to depreciate it.

A Porsche is never *cheap* to buy. It is possible, particularly in the years to come, however, to make it an inexpensive car to own. The same dollars that go into operating and maintaining any automobile become a substantial cost when that car declines in value like last season's new shoes. Those same dollars amount to much less when, in spite of use and the passage of time, the automobile actually retains or increases its value.

> As *Christophorus* editor Reinhard Seiffert put it, "Age and mileage do not play such an important role when we consider the resale price of a car with high life expectancy."

To *invest* in a car one has to choose the *right* automobile. Porsche has proven itself as worthy of time and consideration as a well-located piece of real estate. A recent five-year study of the depreciation of foreign cars, as described in *Money* magazine, placed the Porsche substantially ahead of Mercedes-Benz and BMW in percentage of value retained. Predictably, performance as an investment in the years ahead will only reconfirm the results reported from this survey. Tony Hogg, Editor-in-Chief of *Road and Track,* observes:

> "In the real estate business, they have a saying that the three most important factors when buying are *location, location* and *location,* on the grounds that good locations are always desirable and usually have an increasing scarcity value. Therefore, they are the most likely to increase in value and they tend to have a built-in resistance to any economic downturn. When investing in cars, one can say that the three rules are to buy *quality, quality* and *quality . . ."*

Not every owner views his Porsche as an investment or maintains it with the objective of turning a profit at resale. "It's an awkward subject. One dislikes admitting the financial appreciation of certain cars because it attracts the wrong sort of people, the *investor* rather than the *enthusiast*," admits Allan Girdler, early Speedster enthusiast and a contributing editor to *Automobile Quarterly*. Some devout owners simply intend *never* to sell their cars.

Inflationary factors built into the present U.S. economy, however, automatically transpire to evaluate every Porsche continuously. As a result, just about any Porsche can provide several years of pleasurable driving — to say nothing of status — after which a sale will return a sum at par with the earlier outlay.

For blue chip investment purposes, collectors generally express a preference for the open cars — those Speedsters, Cabriolets and Targas that represent lower production models of the past. Certainly soft tops generally, as a vanishing species, will be among the most desirable cars to own. But as all styles advance in age, the most sterling original examples of the marque will probably be found among the larger populations of coupes. Untouched by scorching sunlight, unexpected rainstorm and heavy night air these will be the individual cars that may even continue to *smell* like new.

As the across-the-board strength of the used Porsche market has attested for many years, there is always someone who wants every particular Porsche offered and is willing to outlay current market value to own it, regardless of body style.

This **Porsche Owner's Companion** has been prepared to amplify interest in any new, original or well-restored car by detailing the action required to maintain its high caliber. While preventative maintenance is proposed in comprehensive outline in the original *Owner's Manual,* it is how piously this program is actually adhered to over the miles that distinguishes the beautiful example of the marque some five, ten or fifteen years after tomorrow.

The owner is well acquainted with the fact that *greater originality spells greater value*. The older the model happens to be, the more premium the enthusiast places on points of originality. Each Porsche first took form on a West German workbench under the hands of craftsmen combining skill and pride to finish it by hand.

Years of use later, however, wear and tear contribute a negative patina requiring corrective action. Each decision and each action in the course of maintenance from Day One contributed to an unique service record. As a result each car becomes highly individual in various details with time's toll. Occasion, place and necessity, governed the nature and extent of each service rendered. A strict continuity of authenticity in replacement over the course of this aging process later distinguishes the outstanding car from others once analogous in production.

The owner's key to enjoying the Porsche Experience is being master of his car's fate rather than permitting it to determine his. Any rear-engine Porsche owner would be hard-pressed if forced to arbitrarily replace his car with a substitute chosen from today's new car marketplace, considering fully the practicality, drivability, safety and comparable assurance of long-term value inherent in his original choice. It certainly follows that awareness and care are required to preserve those attributes that are especially appreciated. Minor corrective action in the beginning will eliminate the need for compound action after neglect.

A prime consideration in work on the Porsche is the dollar compromise for material and craftsmanship to perform a job that provides only a transitory correction. Marginal improvement should be rejected in favor of spending that extra dollar that will assure reconstitution of archival quality. Prescribe perfection. If you are ordering restoration of your right fender from a minor skirmish with everyday realities for your *Eight* on the *Ten* scale 912, don't authorize an *Eight scale* restoration. Order a *Ten* scale job. Overall appreciation or depreciation lies in the balance.

As more Porsches chronologically attain collector status, professional car collectors who never looked twice at Porsches before have entered the scene. As prices of late and new models rise dramatically each year, the solid 356 or 900 series car presents itself worthy of preservation as an investment more than ever before.

As time passes fewer and fewer vintage Porsches in "factory prime" condition remain. The owner of such a prize might well regard restoration beyond normal maintenance as a foolish act. He may have a point. Permitting a car to remain original while experiencing the joys of regular use can be more rewarding. Once left to go downhill — however peerless the finesse applied in the later restorative effort — there will be one car fewer in number on the next roll call of *original* Porsches.

20

Before taking a well-running original car off the road to schedule *carte blanche* major restoration in a concerted sweep, the owner should question if the result will produce a better Porsche, or one having only more "glitter and shine." Unnecessary replacement — substituting a new authorized part for a good used original condition part — has sometimes become an obsession, leaving little time for the owner to enjoy his car. If the object becomes recasting the Porsche as a piece of jewelry, will this owner still be able to use it once he succeeds in transforming it into a "charm?"

It might be more permanently rewarding for him to consider budgeting 15% or 20% of his car's market value *per annum* in a milder upgrading plan that allows use and pleasure with the Porsche along the whole route back to showroom condition.

With ownership the focus pans to the particular year and model in possession and interest intensifies as close-up inspection inspires a challenge.

Compiling a body of reference material relating specifically to this particular acquisition then becomes a scholarly synthesis. The collection properly begins with the appropriate *Owner's Manual.* The manufacturer also offers a number of specialized additional publications that can prove indispensable with ultimate detail carried in the *Porsche Technical Specifications,* volumes pouring forth a virtual cornucopia of measurements and tolerances.

Profiling preservation and restoration progress with your Porsche through the assembly of a contemporary file can be a pleasure with the wit of necessity. Work records that document past service and signal preventative chores form a base. Photographs can be added to delineate unusual details or special before-and-after situations. Sale offers from the classified ad section of the area's principal metropolitan daily newspaper realistically track replacement costs. This program of periodic clipping of pertinent ads not only will chart the actual ongoing valuation of a particular model, but will establish a foundation of reference for the moment in the future when the car may be offered in the market.

When independent supplier parts catalogs, typically available from Stoddard Imported Cars, International Mercantile, Automotion, PB Tweeks, Performance Products and others, are judiciously read, some sections offer a breadth of knowledge above and beyond product descriptions. Reference to these catalogs will keep the owner one-up in the parts availability picture, reward him with leads on further information sources and even provide qualified opportunities for correspondence (see Appendix). Chuck Stoddard of the firm listed above is generally acknowledged as among the foremost Porsche restoration experts in the U.S.

A primary action to extend experience with the car is affiliation with the Porsche Club of America, known as PCA. This non-profit association dates its origin back to the time when the first Porsches were brought into this country. PCA, the largest single *marque* sports car club in the world, is divided into more than 100 local regions, each with its own program of social events, competitions and newsletters. Extending and protecting the owner's best interests is the PCA's excellent monthly magazine, *Porsche Panorama*. National services to render assistance with mechanical and other problems are also provided. For membership information write: Porsche Club of America, P.O. Box 10402, Alexandria, VA 22310.

A second organization also worthy of consideration is the Porsche Owners Club, Inc., or POC, which offers similar benefits on a more regional scale. For information: Porsche Owners Club, P.O. Box 54910, Terminal Annex, Los Angeles CA 90054.

2
THEFT

Murray wedged his flawless 911T into the crowded parking structure's last available space. Uncharacteristically late for the interview, he bolted anxiously for the elevator.

It had taken months for Murray's editor to secure this appointment with a rising young producer whose recent well received releases had made him somewhat of an instant figurehead in the entertainment industry. Murray's magazine had even bent ordinarily unbendable copy deadlines so he could develop this timely subject into a headline feature.

Arriving out-of-breath at the producer's reception desk, he was relieved to learn that Mr. J. had himself been set back and would not be available for another hour.

Reluctantly turning his attention away from the alluring receptionist, Murray decided to obtain additional back-up cassettes for his recorder that lay waiting within the Porsche.

Moments later, striding toward his unmistakable Tangerine car with its subtle white pinstriping, Murray reacted uneasily when he observed a stranger peering intently at the right side of the 911. Murray glared at the unabashed voyeur as he unlocked the door and by habit disabled the alarm.

"Nice car," complimented the stranger. "I've got a black 'S' — same year — just wanted to see if yours is experiencing similar rust problems at the edge of the cowl . . ."

Murray's frown eased as he selected the tapes and casually surveyed the stranger through the passenger window. Neatly groomed with a closely cropped beard, aviator sunglasses nestled on his forehead, and what appeared to be a leather portfolio case clutched under his arm, the man was in his early 'thirties. He seemed like a nice guy.

Rising back to eye level, Murray offered his hand across the Targa top and exchanged introductions with the rust seeker.

"I'm always leery of people monkeying with my car," he admitted.

"I know exactly what you mean," agreed the man who had introduced himself as "Jim." "Just the other day I caught some character starting to snag my alloys."

Murray regarded Jim thoughtfully, then explained he was waiting to do an interview. He asked if the fellow Porsche enthusiast would like to join him for a quick cup of coffee.

Jim conceded that he had a few minutes to kill and accepted the invitation, observing that the subject *Porsche* was always a ready topic of conversation with him.

As they spoke, Jim revealed that he had graduated from business school in the midwest and had only recently come to California to work as an art director with an advertising firm that remained unnamed. He related he was enjoying his new career direction, while still marvelling at the fast-pace Los Angeles lifestyle.

Conversation inevitably returned to cars. Jim said that he was in the process of choosing an alarm for his "E" and asked for advice. Murray offered general observations and explained the finer points of his own particular system in detail.

Glancing at his watch, Murray realized that his reappointed hour was approaching and excused himself after giving Jim his business card. "Give me a call and let know how you make out," he invited cordially.

The producer was now free and he and Murray settled into conversation easily. Murray conducted himself with new confidence — perhaps relaxed by the interlude of Porsche discussion. The busy executive found himself enjoying the interview and he delayed his next appointment long enough for Murray to fill an extra tape.

As the interviewer left Mr. J's presence in a rather smug state, his eye once more drifted to the chipper young secretary perched at her desk near a window overlooking the parking structure. The measure of her voice indicated she was speaking with a friend on the phone . . .

"Oooh. You should have seen the cute little bright orange Porsh [sic.] with an open top that left here a little while ago," she offered excitedly. "It had the softest white striping!"

Murray's mind raced and his pace quickened as he moved through the foyer . . .

He had just learned the hard way what law enforcement people have always known: In contrast with cartoon depictions and TV dramas, *the real thief rarely looks the part.* He also discovered that the car thief depends upon daylight hours, normal activity and a gullible general public as working advantages.

Somewhere in the United States *at least five cars have been stolen since you began reading this chapter.* Three had doors left unlocked and two of these had keys left in the ignition. Two were well secured and one boasted extensive anti-theft devices. Odds are reasonable that the latter may have been a Porsche.

While Porsche stands only as a mere footnote or asterisk in the charts of auto thefts, the percentage of Porsches that are stolen has been estimated to be greater than the percentage of any other production automobile.

No measure short of mustering the service of a "plain-jane" auxiliary vehicle for every excursion when you will not be able to physically guard your Stuttgart jewel will assure anything close to optimum theft protection. In reality you may find yourself no fonder of the "go-for" machine than the potential car thief who will certainly shun it. Consider too that extensive reliance on this stand-in car would tend to negate the very pleasurable experience of owning and maintaining a Porsche.

So it is that the dedicated Porsche driver must be resigned to venture forth into the real world, fully conscious that there is probably less danger lurking in dark shadows than in bright sunshine. The typical car thief is never a night owl with a black domino stretched across beedy eyes. Day by day the Porsche enthusiast enjoys his car, resigned that "it is better to love and lose than never to have loved at all."

Odds are increased in favor of the owner who determines to know the thief he hopes never to meet and acts in certain ways to deter this crook from plying his nefarious craft.

Those with designs on your Porsche are out there, *in numbers,* and they are not about to go away. Every fifteen minutes somebody rips off a car in Los Angeles County alone. The average time for a Porsche left on the street in Brooklyn, New York, before it disappears has been reported in TIME as about 20 minutes. Nationwide, an estimated average of *one of every 145* registered motor vehicles *will be stolen.* In 1978, there were 991,611 such thefts in the U.S. Translation: *one every 32 seconds.* FBI statistics project that more than one million cars were stolen in 1979. The Justice Department conservatively estimates the cost to consumers at $4 billion annually.

Vehicular theft has increased a stunning 500 percent in the last 25 years. During this same quarter century, U.S. population has increased only about 40 percent with new car registrations rising approximately 200 percent.

Somewhere this very hour a clandestine act is demonstrating that it takes less than 30 seconds for a pro to open a locked Porsche, start it, and drive it away. Within 48 hours, this car may assume a new serial number and title papers and may even be in the hands of a new "owner," the fact not withstanding that stolen property never transfers title. One theft ring was actually found to be placing For Sale ads in the newspapers before picking up cars to correspond with the offers.

In recent times, some thieves have shown less interest in a whole Porsche *per se,* than in the sum of its parts. In the black market, these parts become jewels that sometimes bring more cash than the running automobile. Many Porsche parts and accessories are virtually untraceable, while increasing in value as the cars rise. [Illustrated page 26]

Even when a thief does not make off with the car, he may have taken registration papers, license plates, or the Vehicle Identification Number (VIN) plate — the key to establishing title — to cover the theft of another Porsche.

Three quarters of all stolen Porsches are eventually recovered. But that is small consolation when you realize that 70% of these are only body shells picked clean of their assemblies and the garnish

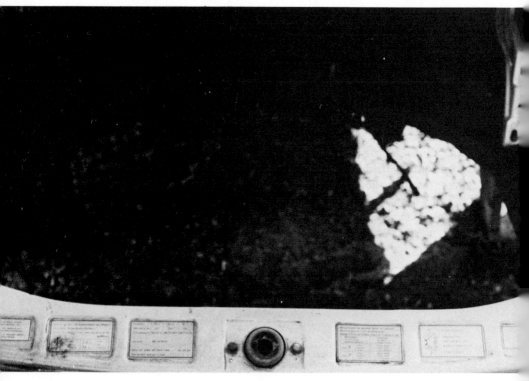

that the trade calls "candy." The Los Angeles Police Department reports that one out of three Porsches recovered in its jurisdiction is "valueless" when found. [Illustrated page 28]

If your Porsche is recovered, national law enforcement statistics indicate that it will most likely be located in the first 48 hours after disappearance. As the number of thefts rises, the rate of recovery drops. This can be attributed to the growing skill of professional thieves and more directly to the receptive market for stolen Porsches among American, European and South American traders who purchase cars without insisting on certificates of title.

Illicit traffic in the Porsche and its parts has become a profession among thieves who sometimes employ elaborate tools. A pro with a portable hydraulic jack uses only two minutes to make off with four alloys. A complete engine extraction seldom takes more than ten minutes. [Illustrated page 28]

The risks inherent in *breaking into* a car can be avoided. Some operators are so well equipped they simply pull up in beautifully maintained tow trucks and, appearing convincingly professional, haul the prize away to meet new friends.

The broader the daylight and the more crowded the area, the simpler the tow-away ploy becomes. The general public is so conditioned to seeing Porsches parked in non-conforming ways that ironically, people assume a car was not complying with an ordinance when they see an undamaged vehicle being cranked up behind a wrecker.

When you drive a Porsche, your car is the target not only for the lone wolf opportunist but a bevy of highly organized specialists. An estimated 40% of all Porsche thefts are the product of smooth-working rings. These operations are not only equipped, but extremely knowledgeable. The efficiency they apply to their trade can be frightening. What they need they have. Working portfolios have been found to include not only counterfeit Vehicle Identification Number plates but also engine serial numbers, EPA certificates, state titles and registration certificates.

Porsche theft operations have become very selective. Recently, one ring searched for the white 924 it needed, apparently to fill an "order." After observing a likely candidate they used the license number to contact the state motor vehicle licensing bureau and determine the owner and his address. By calling him and expressing a convincing interest in purchasing a new 924 just like his, a ring member was able to obtain the name of the dealer from whom the car was purchased. Next, posing as the legitimate owner of the car, a smooth-talking confederate called the dealer and reported that he had lost his keys. When he requested the key identification numbers to facilitate the making of a replacement set the dealer complied.

The 924 was taken from the owner's driveway in broad daylight the next day.

A variety of methods are commonly employed to enter a locked Porsche. The particular approach selected is largely contingent upon the dexterity and resourcefulness of the thief. Only a rank amateur elects to gain entry by breaking a window. Most novices recognize that such an act is too disorderly to be inconspicious.

The method of entry best known to the public utilizes an innocent metal coat hanger reformed into a long, straight wire with an open loop at the working end carefully shaped with an inside diameter just over the size of a door lock button. This easily fashioned tool is forced through the rubber molding at some point around the window and manipulated to unhook a vent wing latch or draw up the door lock.

A less legendary technique for unauthorized entrance utilizes a set of screwdrivers of graduated lengths, each bent at 90 degrees from its handle. When skillfully inserted by the thief, these specially formed tools provide maximum leverage to force the door lock button to unlatch.

The most experienced Porsche thieves use a specialized tool sometimes called a "slim-jim." Fabricated versions of these utensils have been purchased over-the-counter from certain locksmiths, but most have been products from the thieves' own workbenchès. This razor blade-thin tool, also known as a "lock-jock", is sometimes legitimately employed by emergency road services in aiding the "lockout" victim. In use it is maneuvered down into the door panel between the weatherstripping and window glass to the known location of the door latch. After hooking in, the slim-jim is withdrawn in such a way that the locking mechanism becomes disengaged.

Skilled thieves have boasted that one of the speediest ingressions uses a slide hammer, a trade tool primarily used by body and fender workers in pulling out dents in sheet metal. Commonly referred to as a "slamhammer," or "slaphammer," this device is similar in appearance to a large screwdriver. A heavy weight moves freely between the limits of a central shaft, on the order of a doctor's weighing scale. A sheet metal screw is chucked into the business end. After the thief threads this into the lock he thrusts the weight away from the lock toward the handle end of the shaft. When the weight hits its limit in the handle a force is created like a hammer striking away from the surface rather than toward it. This operation can remove the lock cylinder from the door in ten seconds or less.

Less destructive strategies involve key punches which produce instant "slave keys" with the aid of a locksmith's keyway decoder which is used to indicate the depth of the cut needed for a particular lock. A mechanical pick called a "rake gun" is sometimes employed. This device basically resembles a staple gun but uses a thin protruding blade to progressively release pins and tumblers when vibrated by a deft hand.

Once inside, comfortably settled in *your* Recaro and secure from immediate observation, a thief assesses the situation. If a warning sticker indicates an alarm system, he may attempt to disarm that as a first step. The ignition system in early Porsches, designed in a more carefree era, is simple to bypass with mini-alligator clips and jumper wires — and sometimes even tin foil. The common procedure for getting underway in a later car is to use the slaphammer to extract the ignition switch and replace it with a special unit carried for this purpose. Other methods include use of the handy key punch to fabricate a workable key.

Records show that when a professional wishes to take your car, he will. Porsches continuously vanish from locked garages and high security buildings. As the veteran auto theft detail lieutenant observed, "You can slow a pro down, but there is no way to make your car completely theft-proof."

It is not a fluke of nature that a flower as magnificent as a rose carries thorns on its stem. Most would agree that they are there for a reason. The thorns do not always protect the rose from undue abuse, but they are a *deterrent*.

Practicing thieves probably know more about alarm and lock systems than you do, but the touches you have privately added in

locating switches and combining systems may take a little time to figure out. The typical thief is a lazy individual. If you make it difficult and *time consuming* for him at the scene, he might abandon the project and move on to a less-protected mark.

It is taken for granted that you always take the key out of the ignition and lock your doors when you leave. Assuring your Porsche's presence when you later return involves much more. Thwarting the would-be thief can be most effectively managed with a system devised *personally* to assure one-of-a-kind protection. With some imagination and consideration of a combination of general options, you should be able to devise a reasonably sophisticated security system. Unusual placement of components and controls will boost its working security.

Anti-theft devices range from simple padlocks, shut-off switches and valves integrated into the electrical and fuel systems, to complex on-board computerization programmed to override circuits, lock doors, sound alarms and flash lights. The absentee owner may even receive signals by a beeper. Basically there are three areas for consideration: *locks, disabling devices* and *sound units*.

One of the most effective anti-starting measures, and also the least expensive, entails removal and relocation of the rotor and/or coil wire. Realistically, this still permits the car to be rolled or towed away, as well as removal of individual parts from the static vehicle. If you decide to pull either of these motor components on a regular basis, a clean handling system consisting of a glove and parts container should be effectively concealed on the car to facilitate greaseless encounters.

LOCKS

If the car rolls on alloys, it is essential to employ at least one locking lug nut on each wheel. [Illustrated page 32] Certain models of these commonly available locks are also adaptable to other desirable assemblies such as your seats. Demand among parts traders for simple components like tail light lense covers is substantial. You can slow up unauthorized removal by putting liquid wood, Permabond, or a similar compound inside one or two of the holes before reinserting the fastening screws. [Illustrated page 32] This will curtail easy removal with a Yankee screwdriver and

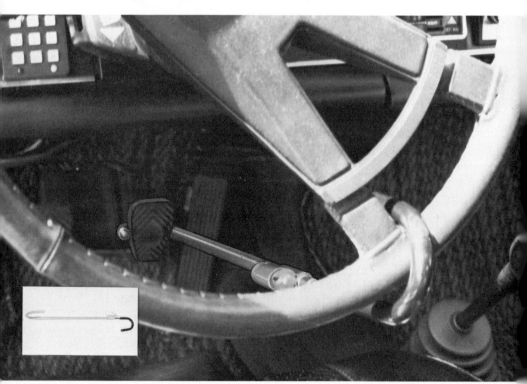

usually forces the thief to exert greater physical pressure and leverage — thereby provoking the motion detector into sounding your alarm.

If you have a vintage coupe with the standard interior hood latch lever, the additional security of a Targa's locking unit is worthwhile. Strippers are further discouraged by unobtrusive padlocks and latches securing vulnerable components such as the spare tire. [Illustrated page 34]

Shackle locks designed specifically for Porsches — and others readily adaptable — have been devised and made available through specialized suppliers. These collars and bars can be set to secure the parking brake in the up position, link the steering wheel to the brake pedal or lock the seat against the wheel. The driver of a Porsche built prior to 1970 without the security of a steering lock may choose from a variety of bars and cables, as well as factory-provided options. [Illustrated page 34] Unfortunately, the availability of some of these very special devices has suffered some inconsistencies because of virtually custom production volume and the limited distribution provided by some small shops. These types of locks are worth investigating. Start with a large auto supply house. Underscored is the importance of improvisation with locks to incorporate an unknown quantity or an added complication whenever possible. One lock-on-a-lock possibility might utilize one of the more sophisticated cable-type bicycle and motorcycle chains or an equivalent measure.

A proven method of preventing unauthorized tow-away entails installing a brake system lock that splices into the hydraulic line. A product requiring the high security tubular type key for release has been built by Sta-Lok. Many 356's were initially equipped with an effective shift lever lock. After the discovery that few people, unfortunately, made use of this security measure it was discontinued.

Any type of locking device carries a two-fold effect. The *visible presence* of the deterrent is generally as discouraging to a potential thief as its actual *function*. He knows that its existence will cost him dangerous extra time before getting under way. Locking devices are particularly effective when used in conjunction with other anti-theft elements.

DISABLING DEVICES

One of the surest measures to slow down a thief is use of an ignition-kill system. This interrupts the voltage supply necessary to turn over the engine and requires a second, remote switch to be activated before the car will start. Inexpensive variations require that a fuse be replaced after an unauthorized starting attempt. You can install a visible toggle switch right at the coil or conceal it with considerable ingenuity. [Illustrated page 36] If you are electrically oriented and can make the installation privately, possibilities will be great. If not, your security will be limited only by the selection of available kits and by the integrity of your installer.

Out-thinking the thief when choosing a location presents real challenge. Make the switch convenient for some private reason beyond the realm of the ordinary. The average burglar rarely has to look farther than under the door mat to find a house key. Strive to disappoint his automotive counterpart by a touch of *illogic*. Consider that a location requiring as little exposure of wiring as possible is going to be less readily located and less vulnerable.

Owners generally consider the challenge of developing a unique and clever installation of compelling adventure and wind up installing a secondary system as well. Excellent locations for secret switches and remote buttons abound in and about your Porsche which can appear stock even after an activating button has been placed behind.

Treating this form of armoring your car lightly may lead to your *next* Porsche being the one you defend effectively.

Specific placement recommendations are withheld in these pages because publication would eliminate the unknown element so essential to security. As a catalyst for your imagination, however, think about the switches already existing on the dash area that you may not currently use. Non-smokers have a variety of options. The glovebox is not a bad location when fed by concealed wiring. [Illustrated page 36]

The crook must first determine that the car has a cut-off switch engaged, then he must weigh the need to look inside a locked dash compartment that doesn't *feel* like it has been wired. If the knob for some ordinary control could be rerouted to another accessory knob or to a hidden spot, then this plain-sight knob could become available as a switch. ON/OFF positions can be reset to mean the opposite. Switch placement is an area in which you have the latitude to make your Porsche *very* personal. Experts concur that imaginative placement of controls is paramount in discouraging theft.

Another category of cut-off stops the flow of gasoline from the tank. With a residual amount of fuel left in the line, pump and/or carburetor, the thief is able to drive away before the Porsche starves out a few hundred yards from the snatch point. Some of the more refined ignition interruption systems have this delaying capability as well. At the point of a mechanical seizure there is a good possibility that the thief will opt to abandon the car on the street, rather than gamble even more time in an attempt to find a hidden switch while exposed to general observation in the midst of traffic.

Residual fuel in the line after making the cut-off enables you to make a change of position in, say, a parking lot without having to be seen handling the switch. Although doing nothing to inhibit the theft initially, such a fuel cut-off certainly increases the chances of recovering the car nearby. These fuel locks, like the electrical cut-offs, are only as effective as their concealment. A system using both a fuel lock and an electrical cut-off would provide maximum protection against all but the pros with their pseudo-wreckers or covered vans.

ARMS

To protect your investment against tow trucks, would-be strippers and everyday vandals, some sort of noise-making system is required. The more obnoxious the sound it emits, the more likelihood it will have of being effective.

Realistically, the burglar alarm installation may prevent your Porsche from establishing residence in another habitat without your consent. The emphasis is on the word *may.* What just about any burglar alarm will do for *certain,* regardless of price and manufacturer's claims, is add to the complexities of your life with your car. In a fashion, the alarm is a necessary evil. Its very sensitivity is its strongest point, but this is a feature you will have to practice living with. With care and skill, you'll find you won't trigger the alarm accidentally every time you get into the car. But prepare to be embarrassed occasionally when you are nearby without the cut-off key in hand. You are the captain of your ship till you leave your alarm in charge. Then your car has a new skipper and it takes eternal vigilance on the part of the owner to remember this. Nonetheless, a theft alarm is a kind of insurance you won't want to do without.

Persistent Porsche pirates have gone to shrewd lengths to get their hands on a car meeting their particular demands. Consider the experience of an east coast attorney who was entertaining dinner guests when his newly installed alarm began to shriek. Quickly excusing himself from the table he moved swiftly down to his Porsche. Finding nothing out of the ordinary, he reset the unit, surmising that the newness of his system might have caused it to trip without provocation.

As the dessert was being served, the alarm began to emit its high-low message once again. Accompanied now by one of his more curious visitors, he took another look at his car and together they combed over it thoroughly in search of a flaw in the alarm system. No evidence of attempted entry or manipulation was found. Again he re-armed the device and returned to the party.

Less than a quarter of an hour later the alarm went off yet again. While a couple of good friends evidenced some concern, others present began to view it as an annoyance and several disparaging comments were heard. Perturbed now by the repeated inconvenience of what was settling in his mind as a defective system, the Porsche owner ran to the car and silenced the alarm *once and for all,* putting it on his mind's agenda to have it checked after his golf game the next morning. Finally he fell asleep that night from the exhaustion of coping with those repeated interruptions which had negated the whole calm atmosphere of the evening.

He never made it to the first tee. The usually stoic lawyer was red-faced as he explained to an investigating officer how the Cashmere SC had disappeared without a whisper sometime during the night though it was equipped with an elaborate and expensive burglar alarm.

The Porsche owner can install all the best locks, cut-offs and alarms that are obtainable, but *unless they are regularly put into service they are all valueless.* No device has yet been designed to shackle the intruder in the vicelike grip of a "beartrap," though it probably wouldn't be a bad idea if one were developed that would have this capability. The best of systems is effective in another manner: it works to startle the burglar and to alert bystanders to the fact the car is being tampered with.

Since it has become increasingly acceptable in contemporary society for the private citizen to abstain from involvement even when he is witness to a criminal act, there is no guarantee against your Porsche sounding its alarm, blowing its horn, ringing its bells and flashing its lights until the battery goes dead. Criteria for selecting a system should include the capability of shutting off automatically after one to five minutes, with automatic resetting. This function will prevent unnecessary battery drain and reduce other inconvenience.

When you hear the alarm or are alerted by a paging device, the first action should always be to alert police to the theft in progress with a car description. Then there is time to attempt to put the criminal under observation or see to it that he flees empty-handed. *Confrontation is not recommended* and could result in more than you bargain for. An alarm will not even bother the car thief with nerves steeled to stand the noise and public attention it has aroused. He knows from experience that his chances of apprehension are slim and especially so for the first minutes of his act. A discouraging 15 percent of all motor vehicle thefts were cleared by arrest of the offenders in 1978.

Not every alarm will signal a theft attempt. It may also deter those who would sit on your fenders and hood. This rather than theft inhibiting is one of the most acclaimed benefits of such a system among Porsche purists.

Three primary types of alarms are currently offered. The least expensive simply utilizes the car's existing horn system as the noise device. A step above this is the bell system that is generally more audible than the horn, while being more conservative in its consumption of battery current. Unfortunately, the bell sound may not attract more than passing public attention even among the more well-intentioned. The loudest, most expensive systems emulate siren noise. While drawing the most current, this sound is more likely to attract the right kind of response from this same public. The siren sound is, however, unlawful for private party use in many areas, being reserved for emergency vehicles use only. European hi-lo sirens can be substituted in states which restrict siren oscillation to emergency vehicles.

40

Alarms can be wired to be activated in a number of ways, depending upon your demands and the limitations of a particular system. Superior Porsche hook-ups seem best provoked by pressure sensitive buttons at the hood and deck lid and by sensing a current drain when a door opening triggers the interior light switch. The practical system incorporates a 10 to 20 second convenience delay after the door is opened to permit the owner to enter and disarm his system.

Activation of the alarm should also be set up through a strategically arranged motion detector, a device designed to set off the system from any undue undulation. An advantage with this device is that the intruder need not gain physical entry to activate the alarm. Jacking, prying, or even the nudging from a minor parking contact between two bumpers will set it off.

Motion detectors vary significantly. They range in size from one square inch mercury switches to weighted swing arms over a foot in length. A few can be used in combination at front and rear. Other delicate numbers must be adjusted very carefully to avoid tripping by heavy winds or the buffeting created by passing traffic, even at their most insensitive settings. Others, adjusted to maximum sensitivity, will not respond to a comparatively light tilt, such as the weight of a body sitting on a fender. Ideally, you should seek a motion detector providing broadly adjustable sensitivity and a switch to deactivate it independently of other alarm functions. This switch will reduce complications that might arise in strong wind conditions or in parking on a grade.

Alarm protection should not be dismissed on the assumption that the thief can be home free simply by cutting a wire or disconnecting a battery cable. Alarms can be built to continue to function even with their wires cut. In practice the average thief will not be in a position to take the time to do this at the beginning. A double set of cables can provide extra protection, with backup wires running from the battery starter terminal to the alarm relay and from the ground terminal to the electrical ground. You also may consider the use of two separate battery systems, each with its own complete wiring. The mounting of a second battery is simplified in the 1969-74 series cars in which a second well has been provided on the opposite side.

When you choose a manual switch-on alarm, the complication from having two or three variously located anti-theft switches calls

for heavy exercise when leaving the car or getting under way. The fact that your passenger would be witness to your unique routine might also occasionally register as a negative factor.

Making it difficult for the driver may also make it difficult for the intruder. However, when multiple switches are assigned, starting your car can become a labor defeating much of the sporting spontaneity so enjoyed by the Porsche owner.

Ingenuity and clean installation of a relatively simple system may offer as much protection as an elaborate number of components that tend to take the fun out of the game.

For convenient activation, the least demanding of alarm systems entails wiring directly to the ignition switch. With this connection you activate the alarm automatically every time you turn off the ignition, or may optionally disarm it by simply turning the key to the accessory position and back. All aspects considered, this presents perhaps the most practical switch solution when a car is in everyday use.

Though it may be considered a sacrilege to drill a hole through the body, many Porsche owners advocate the tubular key-operated external switch. [Illustrated page 42] Its conspicious presence acts in itself as a natural deterrent. When installing a key switch, a stainless steel back-up plate should be used for security, even though the tubular lock is not as readily subject to extraction by slaphammer.

Others who install key switch controls either cannot bring themselves to condone a hole in a visible contour of the body or believe the system should be wholly concealed. They locate the key control under a fender. While aesthetically more acceptable, this introduces several drawbacks. Namely: awkward access, blind handling particularly after dark, an occasionally clogged keyway and, inevitably, muddy hands and clothes in inclement weather.

When choosing an external key switch, it is probably wiser to locate it so it will be visible. This should discourage all but the boldest thieves and, in theory, prevent unnecessary window-breaking and lock and latch disfiguring.

Another visible device to consider is the installation of a dummy switch in which the hookups do not really lead to the alarm relay. Reasonably obvious in its location,this would be discovered early by the thief. As a slowing measure, it would make it necessary for him to go through the steps to disarm the vehicle only to find that he had been taken in by a decoy system. At that point, with time running short, he might abandon his attempt. Misleads may take other forms, such as warning stickers placed prominently in windows to announce an elaborate alarm system that may not be present, or one that may assume a counteracting form. When stickers truthfully declare an alarm-armed Porsche, there is always the possibility that mischievous minors or envious adults might elect to set it off just for the sake of inconveniencing the owner.

Some newer systems offer remote control activation and deactivation by application of a unit working on ultrasound or microwave bands similar to those used in garage door openers. While this might strike you as an ideal arrangement, these controls, which can be operated without a key or other switch installation on the car, have two drawbacks under current technology: they do not enjoy complete radio code privacy and can be affected by a number of uncontrollable outside influences apart from any action of potential thieves; they are not conveniently portable at times away from the car.

Always make it a practice to check out your special system for full function after the car has been picked up from a service point. Cases have been exposed where unscrupulous mechanics have disconnected alarms. Then, by following the owner home or bird-dogging the Porsche for a ring, they have stolen the car before the owner became aware of an alteration in his system. For this reason it is wise to have an alarm that chirps when you turn it on as confirmation of its effective state.

A sophisticated anti-theft unit particularly popular among Porsche people is the "Ungo Box," made by Techne Electronics. Developed expressly for use in the Porsche, it combines a quality alarm with an effective ignition disabler. Operation is without keys or switches. Inside the magic box, hinged components are wired to spring-loaded sensors set both to trigger a motion alarm and to disable through circuit-breaking. Aside from basic alarm and disabling functions, the unit also provides a manual trigger to activate the alarm in the event that attention or assistance is required in or around the car.

With this unit there is no need to turn the system on when parking. The Ungo Box is always "on," except when deliberately turned off. A ten-second door delay is provided after opening for your entry, with no delay built in for hood and deck lid accesses. The piercing alarm is programmed to sound for 60 seconds and then reset. If a thief continues to tamper with the car when it shuts down, the alarm will automatically be reactivated for another 60 seconds as many times as required by conditions. A compact beep pager capable of signaling the owner of tampering within a two to four mile range is offered as an Ungo accessory.

While these protective features could be incorporated into any system, the Ungo Box package brings together effective anti-theft measures in a *single* commerical product.

The Box is deactivated by dialing in a combination number from a conveniently located keyboard. More than 10,000 factory-set combinations are claimed possible. Incorrect dialing will set off the alarm.

Compact motion detectors, miniaturized memory chips, digital read-outs, and even a measure of over-design are represented in the Clifford system which may not be within the financial reach of every owner. As with any protective alarm, the dollar investment can be justified when considered in comparison with the increased insurance premiums generally required of an owner who has suffered a theft loss. Authorized dealers usually endorse and install systems featuring state-of-the-art Clifford alarms which are similar to the Ungo Box but offer a more integrated installation while requiring fairly elaborate fitting. Clifford components are mounted ''in dash'' and are most common among more recent production. [Illustrated page 42] The Clifford may be among the most expensive theft deterrent systems obtainable. It is also among the best.

In tailoring your unique combination of components to vie against the forces of evil, the most workable result will be assured by using equipment that already has a track record of effective installations in the Porsche. Beyond this, the boundaries of your personal budget will help to guide you in certain choices.

The trusted technician engaged to install your plan should also be knowledgeable in the peculiarities of this car. Equally important is his integrity. When a stranger is the only one available to do this work, it is sometimes possible to check with the Better Business Bureau or a local Chamber of Commerce. Credentials might also be confirmed by asking a friend in the police department to get an

answer or two about the firm from the police of the city where you are having the installation made.

Like a locksmith, the security system specialist is *supposed* to be a pillar of the business community. Some states require that these professionals be bonded. Nonetheless, there are many cases on record where even certified installers have made clandestine use of their knowledge. Some wariness on your part is critical. One body repair specialist with top marks among insurance companies turned out to be linked to a successful theft ring, from whom he in turn was being supplied with prime sheet metal "used" parts. As it was revealed, the body shop people, acting as "pickers," were acquainting themselves fully with particular personal alarm systems, their functions, and particularly their disfunction, while cars were in their care for restoration services.

FACILITATING RECOVERY

Is your car too distinctive to become a prime target for the professional thief? Convicts interviewed in a prison survey expressed a marked preference for the stock colored, unladen Porsche over one with a special candy color and prominent modifications like louvres, flared fenders, a spoiler or a whaletail. [Illustrated page 46] Even custom pinstriping on a conservative, original car has sometimes been regarded as too readily identifiable to fool with and has prompted the thief to move on. [Illustrated page 48]

Unfortunately, one lawbreaker's poison is another's fancy. The amateur joyrider may be primarily attracted to the Porsche in street racer stance.

While conspicuous customization obviously makes a Porsche easier for the police to spot and recover — and harder for the thief to dispose of — few owners would advocate customizing as an insurance policy. Every single departure from originality must be seasoned by good judgment so the intrinsic value of the car will not be compromised. [Illustrated page 49]

Modifications of less visible nature to the thief, on the other hand, can build in potential benefits for positive identification. Since standard VIN numbers are commonly altered after theft, it is always wise to mark your car in several hard-to-find areas.

VEHICLE REPORT

REGISTERED OWNER (FIRM NAME IF BUSINESS)	CASE NO.
ADDRESS	

☐ STORED
☐ STOLEN ☐ IMPOUNDED ☐ RECOVERED ☐ OUTSIDE RECOVERY

VIN NO.		YEAR	STATE	LICENSE NO.

PLATES LOST/STOLEN
☐ ABANDONED ☐ MISSING PERSON ☐ ONE ☐ TWO

YEAR	MAKE-VEHICLE	BODY TYPE	BODY COLOR(S) OTHER IDENTIFYING FEATURES

REPORTED TO POLICE			CITATION NO.	PERSON REPORTING OCCURRENCE TO POL. DEPT.	SOC SEC/DR. LISCENSE
DAY	DATE	TIME			

IGNITION LOCKED YES☐ NO☐ UNK☐	DOORS LOCKED YES☐ NO☐ UNK☐		STREET DRIVEWAY ALLEY	RESIDENCE ADDRESS		RESID. PHONE	BUSINESS PHONE
KEYS IN VEHICLE YES☐ NO☐ UNK☐	ORIGINAL ENGINE YES☐ NO☐ UNK☐	FROM	CARPORT APT SCHOOL	DATE OF OCCURRENCE	BETWEEN HOURS OF AND	ENG. NO.	
ORIGINAL TRANS YES☐ NO☐ UNK☐	TRANSCRIBED BY		MARKET SHOP CNTR CAR LOT	LOCATION OF OCCURRENCE		OFFICER	BEAT NO.

STORED VEHICLE INVENTORY REPORT

	YES	NO		YES	NO		YES	NO	PROPERTY, TOOLS, CLOTHING, LUGGAGE	FURTHER VEH DESCRIPTION (ANY UNUSUAL FEATURES)
CUSHION (FRONT)			SPOTLIGHT(S)			L.F. TIRE				
CUSHION (REAR)			FOGLIGHT(S)			R.F. TIRE				
REAR VIEW MIRROR			BUMPER (FRONT)			R.R. TIRE				
SIDE VIEW MIRROR			BUMPER (REAR)			L.R. TIRE			INSURANCE CO. NAME	
CIGAR LIGHTER			MOTOR			SPARE TIRE				
RADIO			BATTERY			WHEELS			MODIFIED EQUIP (CIRCLE ITEM)	
CLOCK			AIR CONDITIONER			FENDERS			BUCKET SEATS	UPHOLSTERY
HEATER			HUB CAPS			BODY, HOOD			STEREO TAPE VINYL TOP	RIPPED
KEYS			FENDER PARTS			TOP			STEREO SPEAKERS CUSTOM PAINT	CUSTOM
REGISTRATION			TRANSMISSION			GRILL			FLOOR SHIFT	UNUSUAL
WINDSHIELD WIPER			JACK			UPHOLSTERY			DAMAGE WINDOWS	TINTED
GENERATOR			TRUNK LOCKED						LEFT SIDE HOOD	COVERED
RADIATOR			GLOVE COMPARTMENT LOCKED						RIGHT SIDE ROOF	STICKER

LOCATION FROM WHICH TOWED/ RECOVERY INFO | BEAT NO. | RECOVERING OFFICER

FRONT END OTHER — DECAL
REAR END — DAMAGED / CRACKED

CONDITION OF VEHICLE BURNED DAMAGED	ODOMETER READING	CUSTOM PAINT LOWERED RAISED WHEELS CHROME MAGS OVERSIZE

NOTE PORTIONS WRECKED AND STRIPPED

NAME OF GARAGE	ADDRESS	CITY	PHONE NUMBER

NAME OF PLACE VEHICLE IS STORED	LOCATION	TOWED BY

OFFICER ORDERING VEHICLE STORED (SIGNATURE)	GARAGE PRINCIPAL OR AGENT STORING VEH. (SIGNATURE)	DATE	TIME
X	X		

1. IDENTIFY SUSPECTS BY NUMBER. GIVE NAME, ADDRESS, SEX, DESCENT, AGE, HEIGHT, WEIGHT, HAIR, EYES, COMPLEXION, CLOTHING, ETC.
2. IF ARRESTED, GIVE FULL NAME, AGE, CHARGE, DATE, TIME OF ARREST & NAME OF ARRESTING OFFICER. ADDED INFORMATION: (1) CIRCUMSTANCES SURROUNDING OCCURRENCE(S).

FORCED ENTRY OR OTHER	THEFT FROM VEH.	RECOVERY INFO. TRANSCRIBED BY TIME	PLATES CHANGED

HOW BROUGHT IN TOW DRIVE	RUNNING COND. YES NO	OFFICER STORING VEHICLE	VEHICLE TO BE RELEASED HELD	HOLD ORDERED BY	DATE/TIME HOLD ORDERED
OFF. ORDERING RELEASE	DATE/TIME RELEASE ORDERED		AUTO HELD FOR—UNIT AUTO THEFT BURG NARCO HIT-RUN OTHER		
OFF. RELEASING VEHICLE	DATE/TIME VEHICLE RELEASED		PERSON VEHICLE RELEASED TO SIGNATURE X ADDRESS		

DATE/TIME IN AUTO-STATUS	ORDER BY	DATE/TIME RADIO BRDCT. SENT	ORDER BY	OWNER OR AGENCY NOTIFIED BY	DATE/TIME OWNER/AGENCY NOTIFIED
DATE/TIME AUTO-STATUS CANCELLED	ORDER BY	DATE/TIME RADIO BRDCT. CANCELLED	ORDER BY	METHOD T.T. TT PHONE NO.	

FCN _____ / _____ / _____

Dropping a business card down the door's window opening is the recommended secret identification passed down through generations of car owners. There are certainly better places on the Porsche to hide a card that might not require the court order you must have to dismantle a suspect door to see if your card is, in fact, present. Think of a place where you can conceal a card — or a card cut into thin strips carrying the pertinent data — so it will not be exposed in handling or transfer and in parting out, but which will provide access on call. Would a decoy water drain tube give you any ideas? Is your shift lever *hollow?*

As to citing precise locations for concealment, the writer must leave final determination up to the reader so that this book does not provide a check list helpful to the wrong parties.

If the car is recovered after a theft, any such personal touches that the rightful owner can describe will help in making claim, when the car has been modified with substitute numbers and refinishing.

Mark your Porsche liberally in as many locations as present themselves. Consider the body sections separately — the doors, the hood, motor lid and the main shell all can be made individually identifiable. The running gear and engine may also be marked in several spots. *Your own driver's license number, with your state, is probably the most appropriate alphanumeric reference you can use.* An engraving tool, paint, finger nail polish, even a felt-tip pen are all handy for doing the job right. Such unobtrusive markings will do little to *prevent* theft, but they can increase chances of recovery and may aid authorities in securing theft convictions. Imagine establishing a claim by scraping away some thick undercoating on a rocker panel to reveal a firmly fixed Dymo label you had the foresight to implant on an earlier occasion.

Some Porsche enthusiasts have fabricated unique templates with irregular hole patterns which they have then used to stencil with paint, or drill or punch, so the one-of-a-kind pattern is transferred to the car in an unlikely area. Matching the template to the car you claim as yours can provide dramatic and conclusive proof to everyone present at that later moment when it might prove appropos.

In the event your Porsche or any of its parts are stolen, you will find that *being able to produce a list of identifying numbers for law*

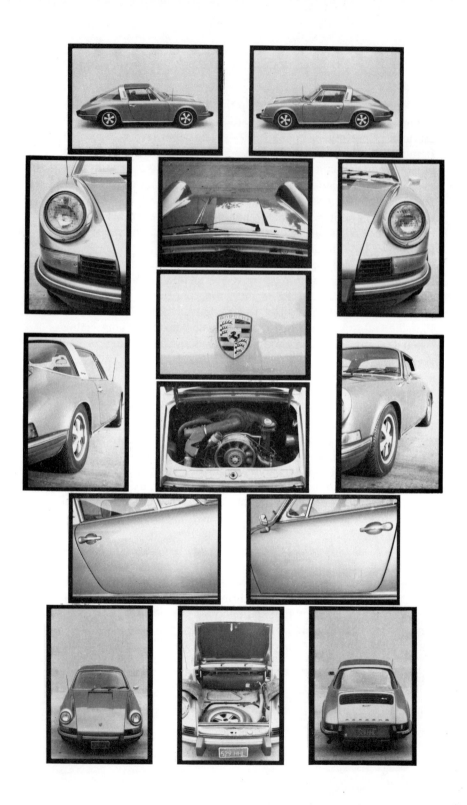

enforcement to work with will make a great difference. You, and anyone else driving your Porsche, should carry complete data on the year, model, license plate number, VIN, and as many accessory serial numbers as can be mustered in a list. The best place to carry this form is right next to your driver's license in your billfold. The form that follows may be used as a guide. [Illustrated page 54] Worth your time, before the theft, would be a little photography session, with the car being covered from various angles. Try to record any points that make your particular car unique. If your Porsche carries a body section or some spot that digresses in form from the contour it had when it left Stuttgart, give thought to recording this micro-peculiarity that makes it one-of-a-kind for identification purposes. Before nine o'clock in the morning and after five in the evening are probably the best times to secure the flattest natural reflections for recording such highlight detail.

A wise Porsche owner would never leave his license, registration or other identification in the car, unless the state he is driving in requires it. (Even then, consider carrying only a Xerox copy.) Any matter of this nature could help a thief to create an illusion of ownership. Even when he enters but does not make off with the car, an unknown toll may have been taken. He may have ripped off registration papers, or VIN and other plates to cover the theft of another Porsche with like specifications.

Although superficially more of an inconvenience for the owner than an outright loss, the theft of license plates should not be taken lightly. A set of clean tags on a hot car can assure the thief additional hours of "safe" operation. Sometimes, thinking the owner might be slow to notice the switch, the thief *substitutes* license plates, leaving a hot set in exchange so the car remains complete. An habitual glance at your plates every time you approach your car is the best insurance against complications in this quarter.

IN RECAPPING

Unless you are one of those individuals who would leave his keys in the Porsche anyway after having gone to great lengths to arm it against theft, you may skip the rest of this paragraph. Cliché as it sounds, enticing property — cameras, sports equipment, luggage or an attaché case — should never be left visible in the

Porsche Owner's Serial Specs for the Pocket

Description & Title

Model_____ Type_____ Year_____

Body Style_____ VIN _____

Engine Number _____ Transmission _____

Color_____ Paint Number _____

License Plate_____ State _____

Registered Owner_____

Legal Owner _____

Insurance Carrier _____ Contact _____

Accessories & Special Considerations

Air Conditioning System _____

Radio / Sound Systems_____

Alarm / Deterrent Systems _____

Exterior Accessories_____

Interior Accessories _____

Intentional Secret Identifying Marks _____

Unique Wear and Tear Details_____

Confidential Codes _____

Other _____

Wheel & Tire Specifications

	Alloy Serial	Tire	Size	Tire Serial
LF	_____	_____	_____	_____
RF	_____	_____	_____	_____
LR	_____	_____	_____	_____
RR	_____	_____	_____	_____
SP	_____	_____	_____	_____

cockpit of your car. Valuables should be transferred to the trunk *before* pulling into your destination so an opportunist cannot observe your action.

Enhance security by putting these precautionary measures you know about into practice:

Increasing the Odds

Consider bright colors, pinstriping and unique modification so your Porsche will be easier to spot and harder to dispose of quickly in the subculture. Avoid alterations that would depreciate the car in the legitimate market as well.

Replace the "mushroom" door lock controls with a cylinder type. [Illustrated page 56]

Put a locking nut on each wheel and padlock your spare.

Unobtrusively mark your car with personal identification in as many remote locations as possible. Record all serial numbers and take photographs for your records.

Avoid hiding spare keys somewhere about the car. Experienced Porschenappers know all the right places to look.

Be as wary during the sale as you were during the purchase.

If you have an alarm, remember to set it.

The Preventive System

If you do not have a warning system, get one.

Install a hidden ignition cut-off switch or remove the coil wire.

Install a fuel shut-off valve.

Parking Considerations

[Elaboration pages 95-101]

Avoid dark areas; park on well traveled, brightly lighted streets. Consider a corner or end location so any undue attention directed to the Porsche would be visible from two or more directions.

Break up any pattern of parking so the same space or area is not used on a regular schedule.

When leaving car in a city parking lot, be elusive about how long you will be gone.

Try to keep the car within immediate sight whenever possible.

When Leaving the Car

Never leave important or identifying papers in your car, even personal letter envelopes. Conceal valuables.

Never leave the key in your car even when it's stationed in your personal driveway or garage. When a garage is available, use it.

Always roll up the windows and the doors when you depart. Never leave a crack at the top of the window on a hot day; leave the dash vent open instead. There are those whose definition of "hot car" might differ from your own.

Use the theft prevention devices you have installed.

Carry a cable or bar lock for the steering wheel-to-brake-pedal type of protection and use it if you feel the car is vulnerable, or when you will be leaving it unattended for an extended time.

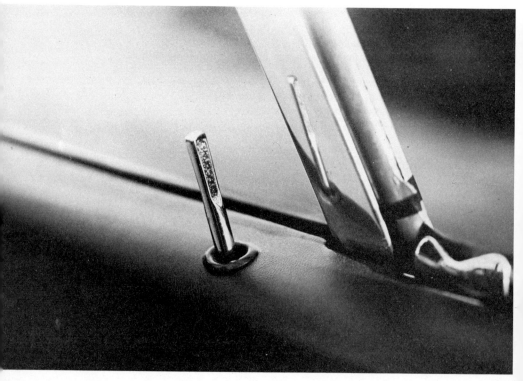

Unfortunately, even a shrewdly developed combination system may prove fallible. A car armed heavily with sophisticated deterrents can, in certain circumstances, serve as a challenge in the stealthy game graduate Porsche thieves play. Feasibly, a narcissist might break in and drive the car a couple of blocks from the scene just to satisfy his demented ego. Such cases have, in fact, been documented. In a 1977 issue, *Car and Driver* spotlighted a thief with a passion for the impossible:

> One Porsche wired with every conceivable anti-theft device took Danny an hour to get into — his worst time. But it was the third Porsche he had lifted from the same owner. The poor guy had added alarms, hidden fuel switches, everything he could think of. After he lifted the third one, Danny says, the man moved out of town.

A happy balance must be reached. Consider your own well being. It is critical not to so over-adorn your car with theft deterrents and complicating control elements that you discover that you no longer *enjoy* driving your car.

SELLING

Marcia adored her 911S. It was the cosmetic mortality the car was incurring in necessary intracity operation that had been bothering her. Now she felt that the car deserved more than she was giving it. Although the purchase of this white '76 symbolized the fulfillment of a dream conceived before she had even acquired a driver's license, immediate financial priorities now forced a revised plan.

Early the week before, in a moment of euphoria, Marcia had contracted to acquire half interest in a beautiful 37 foot sailing vessel, the realization of another long nurtured fantasy. Unfortunately, she had discovered she was not going to be able to keep Peter and still pay Paul. Confronted with an either/or decision, she decided against assuming a second mortgage on her harbor front home and liquidation of her cherished Porsche now represented the balance of her payment due the broker on the first.

After several days of careful detailing, Marcia advertised the "S" in the classified of the Sunday edition of a local paper. Typically, the first caller was eager to see the machine. After a knowledgeable preliminary telephone inquiry, a respectable-appearing young couple — the Smiths — drove out from a "neighboring suburb" to inspect her manicured pride. Pridefully she pointed out the car's obvious integrity to a willing audience. Apparently sold on the car, Smith opened negotiations by offering Marcia almost three thousand less than her asking price. It was a low blow. As calculated by the bidder, this offer was quickly refused, though Marcia was moved to indicate that she would be willing to consider an offer within a thousand dollars of the advertised figure. The two excused themselves politely, claiming they were not prepared to spend that much money. The young lady was still confident that other parties would call.

As it happened, her moment of financial need was not unique. She had unwittingly offered the car for sale at a time when many people were just recovering from IRS blues and the end of April was just ahead. There were several phone inquiries but no other prospects materialized in person.

On Wednesday Marcia received a call from the distaff side of the one party who had come out to look. "Do you still have the car?" Mrs. Smith reconfirmed their interest in the 911 and set up another meeting. Marcia hoped with fingers crossed that this renewed interest might result in the sale. If she had only known then what she was later to learn, it would have been clear that crossing legs, arms and eyes as well would not have changed things for the better.

At the new encounter, the prospects emphasized minor imperfections in the vehicle and attempted to get her to reduce the price substantially. They had brought along a mechanic friend to check out the engine. It was an effort well calculated to convince Marcia of their honest interest in the car, qualified only by limited means. At this point in the negotiations, Marcia reluctantly further acceded to a new minimum selling price. In response, the couple tenuously offered $500 less. Marcia knew her 911 was worth more and stood pat on her previous reduction. They assured her they would be in touch the following day to see if Marcia had changed her mind. As the Smiths parted Marcia tried to fight off an uneasy feeling of being trapped.

Thursday came and the promised call came through. The woman offered to obtain a cashier's check for their previous day's offer if this were now acceptable. In desperation Marcia conceded and an agreement was finally reached. Following the established patterns, an appointment was made for eleven the next morning with Marcia pledging to have her Porsche's title ready for a simple exchange when the couple arrived.

Early Friday morning Smith called and asked whether her name was spelled *Marcia* or *Marsha*. He wanted to have the check made out properly. Two hours later he called again. He reported that the cashier's check had been prepared, but that he would be unable to make the morning appointment on account of an important business conflict. Since two were needed to pick up the car, he changed the appointment to that afternoon. Marcia, now resigned to the unhappy parting, waited patiently for 1:30. As this revised time slot approached, she answered a new call and was apologetically informed that the transaction would have to be postponed until 6:30 that evening.

With this delay, that intuitive sense that had caused uneasiness the night before returned in spades. The spirited girl with too many interests was all too conscious of the fact that the transaction was now designated for a time after banking hours. With this thought she began to question the legitimacy of the Smiths' intentions. The couple was counting on exactly this reaction.

At 6:30 the kicker came, though Marcia was not conscious of the significance of the ploy at the time. Mrs. Smith called to relate how the day had gone awry with complications. It would be impossible for them to make contact that evening, but they would be out first thing in the morning.

This whole series of postponements had been constructed to persuade the girl that had her prospects merely been trying to avoid banking hours they would certainly have managed to keep the evening appointment. As planned by the professionals, Marcia now became more relaxed and trusting. She even thought of apologizing to them, once the exchange had been consumated, for having at one point entertained inner feelings questioning their integrity.

Early Saturday morning the two parties met and closed the deal. After watching her car disappear up the lane Marcia returned to her den and spent a relaxed weekend getting into Maté's *The Finely Fitted Yacht*. Monday morning she deposited the check in her checking account, pending a withdrawal for the sloop.

The next day the bottom fell out of the life Marcia had known. It began with a call from her bank. *The check was a forgery, from the*

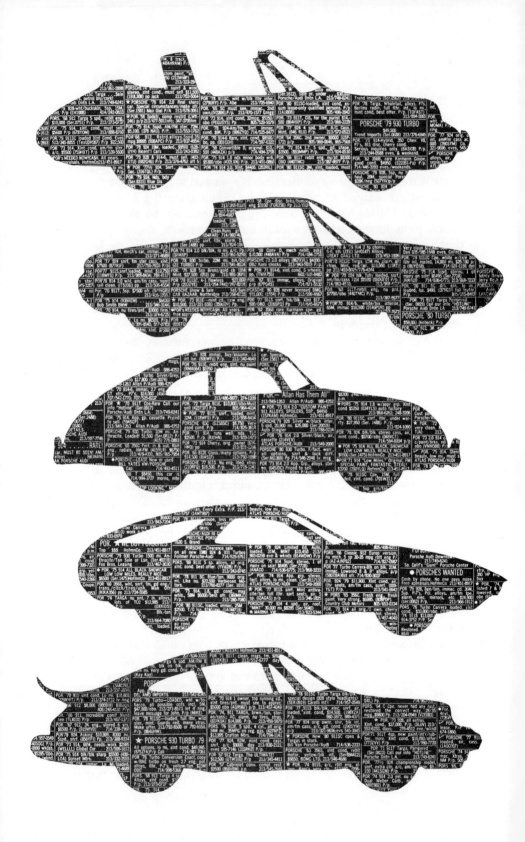

printing to the signature. She had released her Porsche's certificate of ownership days before. The couple had already been permitted several comfortable days of lead time in which to transport or dispose of the 911S.

When the distraught young sportswoman reported details of the swindle to the police that day, they reminded her that the car could already be in another state, or might even have ceased to exist through having been dismantled for parts. The white "S" was never recovered.

While the Porsche owner may be more astute than the average motorist in keeping himself apprised of current price trends, statistics indicate that he is not above being taken in by the well-executed con game. Among the most successful ploys are those surfacing in connection with a sale. Porsche "specialists" are often charming conversationalists, masters of psychology and extremely knowledgeable in matters *Porsche,* as well. They rely on the classified ads in the selection of their prey. Once chosen, the job becomes one of qualifying the mark, or, more literally, determining his or her relative vulnerability.

These people know they are home free when dealing with an owner who would rate One on the Ten Scale for intelligence. But Marcia was no moron and there have been many other Marcias, each just as gently pushed into a situation of disaster. Con men and women, sad to say, so pride themselves on their craft that they have been known deliberately to take on marks much higher on the Scale just to feed their own egos. To such a master of deception, apparently, there is more satisfaction in making a dupe of a rising young attorney than of an image-conscious factory worker.

Only knowledge of the con artist's objectives will protect the owner from becoming a victim. Since these are often deviously obscured during the progress of a scam, it is necessary not to permit certain footholds to be gained in any form. When qualifying a prospective buyer:

1. Take the time to insure a legitimate transaction when handling prospects. Set appointments so that only one party calls to see the car at a given time.

2. Never permit your prospect to call the shots. Try to judge his credibility outside of the story that he may tell. For example, in conversation on common ground, such as a car agency both are acquainted with, try inquiring about a "favorite" mechanic (using a

name you make up on the spot) and determine if the prospect knows of this person.

3. Avoid revealing the fine points of your alarm system from A to Z with every looker.

4. Never permit a prospect to drive off independently in your car for a test drive. *Never.* Some thieves do not have the finesse in their working procedures to con you out of your title so they simply smooth talk you out of your keys. In some states, when the owner gives his permission for another individual to take his vehicle for a test run and the car is not immediately returned, the case becomes a civil offense rather than a criminal one. In this event many police departments find no basis for writing up a theft report.

5. Instead, go with him, or arrange a time for the run when you can accompany him. It is sometimes forgotten that the comparably valued car he drives up in which might influence you favorably as a sort of tacit collateral may, in fact, have been stolen for the very purpose of looking good at your curbside. When time permits, it is good to have the license checked out through your local DMV where a small fee will be charged for this "make" request.

6. When a sixth sense signals that your prospect may *not* be cut from the same cloth as he would have it appear, stay tight; remain in control. Be suddenly, but subtly, more difficult. "Well, I cannot make it Sunday morning. But I can meet you at your bank at 10 A.M. Monday."

7. After setting up a mutually agreeable time for transacting the sale, accompany the buyer to his bank to assure proper compensation, preferably cash.

8. Try to set it up so you can accompany him to the Department of Motor Vehicles directly from the bank, so you may also witness transfer of the car to the buyer. This will confirm that the buyer wants the car for himself and will relieve the seller of potential public liability in the event the transfer with the state was not carried out promptly.

BUYING

Exercising caution in *purchasing* a previously-owned Porsche is as important as in *selling*. Under public law, title to a stolen automobile does not pass on through subsequent hands. Recovery can be made at any time, even years after the original theft. When an enthusiast-restorer is shocked by the discovery that he has purchased a car with a fraudulent title, the hurt has only begun to smart. He may stand to loose not only all the cash and time he has lavished on improvements but the price he paid for the car itself.

The legal rights of the party in possession of a stolen Porsche, however innocently it may have been acquired, are virtually non-existent. All important points of the law favor the true owner. It remains only for him to prove his claim. Special acid etching, electrolytic and heat processes can reproduce altered numbers under laboratory conditions as one aid. Another bears witness to the car's rightful owner if he had the foresight to place secret identifying marks and numbers in unlikely places. All in all the original victim stands to eventually regain possession leaving any subsequent victims simply holding the bag.

Be sure you are looking at a car that is legitimately the property of the party showing it. Tie his name to the car by examining the title. Tie his residence to the place you have gone to look at the Porsche by confirming it with the telephone book. Note on the pink slip how long he has owned the car. Invite him to tell you in detail his experiences with the car and his reason for offering it for sale. If you have any reason to suspect that you are being set up by a "housesitter" return later and confirm the validity of both prospect and his car, by inquiring of his neighbors.

The interstate operator is a thief particularly familiar with the disparity among title laws in neighboring states. He turns this to his advantage. A certificate of ownership is not required in order to license a Porsche in several states. At this writing they include: Alabama, Kentucky, Maine, Massachusetts, Minnesota, New York, Rhode Island and Vermont. Porsches stolen from titled areas can be re-registered with no supporting documentation in these "non-title" states. The sale offer featuring a car with a pedigree from one of these states can bring bad news. Counterfeit titles are surfacing with growing frequency.

One of the problems stems from the fact that forgeries are often prepared with all the advantages of modern lithography and are not detectable as bogus except to the trained eye. According to a manual issued by the International Association of Chiefs of Police, even long-established American car dealers generally accept such titles without question. In turn, employees of state DMV divisions are often so involved in their transfer processing loads that little time is alloted to scrutinizing the finer points of individual documents. Sometimes only the less sophisticated phony is detected. As a result Porsches have occasionally passed through several "owners" before recovery — with subsequent total loss to the title holder of current record.

When a purchase is being considered, *the title paper should be checked for comparison against a like document of established validity.*

The false title is only the tip of the iceberg. This paper has usually been generated from a false identity based on restamped or substituted serial numbers. The prevailing volume of hot cars is reintroduced to the unsuspecting through a laundering process known as the "salvage switch." Professional auto theft rings commonly exchange alphanumeric identification from a clear titled Porsche, most often residing inoperable in a wrecking yard, with that of a stolen car of the same specification profile or one that is close enough to "pass." FBI estimates reveal that as many as 75% of the cars handled by organized rings are disposed of by utilizing some variation of this approach.

Validation of the history of a particular individual Porsche may be made by matching numbers with the pedigree directory listing, reprinted from the *Porsche Family Tree,* a factory publication. These tables provide VIN's engine numbers and body styles, chronologically. Consult this listing [See pages 186-189] whenever you consider a purchase. If you find that the VIN on that inviting ten-year-old Targa actually originated on a later coupe, it will prove a pleasanter discovery *before* consumation of purchase. When time is not of the essence, a very safe procedure involves communicating with the factory to confirm that the VIN in question corresponds exactly in body style, color and date of manufacture with that revealed on the EPA sticker located in the Porsche's door frame.

When inspecting a car for purchase, adopt the habit of noting the manner in which the VIN plate is attached. Be familiar with the *authentic* means of mounting and look for any evidence of discrepancy. Thieves commonly reaffix the all-important VIN by substituting garden-variety pop rivets and some have even used a glue or epoxy cement. Any attachment that evokes suspicion should immediately lay down a red flag on the whole proposition. Walk away from this car while you can.

COMPUTER REPORTS

Computerized hot car and title information is being used increasingly by law inforcement to combat the mammoth menace of car theft. Virtually all investigative agencies in the United States have some access to such systems. It is often possible now in a given situation for a local police department to determine quickly if a particular Porsche is stolen and to locate the name of the registered owner.

THE NATIONAL AUTOMOBILE THEFT BUREAU

The NATB is a non-profit service organization of long standing, supported by a consortium of insurance companies. The NATB maintains coordinated nationwide files of information on stolen vehicles, which list every stolen Porsche, as well as other cars, by year, VIN and owner's name. Records from data reported by member insurance companies are also correlated on "totaled" vehicles which have been sold to dismantlers. By consulting this memory bank in the NATB archives one can first verify that a vehicle was actually produced and then trace it from its factory to its last rightful owner.

Unrecovered vehicle records remain in an active file for five years from the date of theft. Requests for information should be directed to the appropriate divisional office listed here. Each is equipped with printout terminals for access to the Chicago data storage banks.

National Office
390 North Broadway, Room 350
Jericho NY 11753
   Phone 516/935-7272

National Systems Division
9730 S. Western Avenue
Chicago IL 60642
   Phone 312/499-2620

Eastern Division
17 John Street
New York NY 10038
   Phone 212/233-1400

Western Division
9730 S. Western Avenue
Chicago IL 60642
   Phone 312/499-2620

Southwestern Division
1341 West Mockingbird Ln., Suite 1006E
Dallas TX 75247
   Phone 214/630-1666

Southern Division
P.O. Box 95008
Atlanta GA 30347
   Phone 404/633-6305

Pacific Coast Division
1001 Bryant Street
San Francisco CA 94103
   Phone 415-863-2404

Canadian Division
P.O. Box 919, Station "U"
Toronto, Ontario, Canada M8Z 5P9
   Phone 416/252-5215

Experienced Porsche collectors recommend tracing a car all the way back to the original authorized dealer not only to verify numbers but to profile use. State laws are disparate on this point. Some states provide dealer identity on the title; others do not. Very often the dealer's name will be conveniently found as a rubber stamp in the Owner's Manual. Even with immediate access to the dealer's files, it can still prove rewarding to contact previous owners. You may not learn that the car is stolen, but might become aware of other considerations that make the car less desirable. The prospective buyer should be especially wary when evidence is uncovered of a recent transaction involving the same seller and another party — implying a sale that did not go through.

To develop this motor geneology ask the person currently offering the Porsche for sale for the identity of the party from whom he purchased the car. The seller with a clear conscience should make this information readily available. From this previous owner one should obtain a good description of the car as then constituted, including mileage and major repair remarks as well as the name of the next previous owner. In the process of this search back to the original owner a unique dossier will be assembled. Critically, it will either paint a picture of a desirable car or one to be avoided. Experts concur that this enlightenment is invariably worth the detective work it may entail.

3
INSURANCE

Richard had purchased his 912 Targa off the floor in 1969 for roughly one third of what he had just agreed to part with it for — more than a decade later. He was hopelessly set on owning a 928.

Over the years, Richard had adorned his cherished companion with many desirable extras. Leather Recaros and a Blaupunkt integrated component sound system represented two substantial investments and a host of less conspicious amenities included Bilsteins and alloy brake calipers.

Factory original finish had been immaculately preserved and all five wheels were meticulously polished. It had been garaged since Day One. In service the car had seen nothing but dry Southern California roads and its odometer legitimately indicated just over 40,000 weekend miles. Unlike many vehicles of comparable vintage, this one was a stranger to body shop encounters.

Double clutching his downshift with the certainty of total familiarity, Richard drifted into the parking lot of the bank and carefully chose a remote corner parking spot. His passenger beamed in anticipation of owning this pampered machine.

Stifling an urge to spend the time in his Recaro, Richard locked the car and accompanied the buyer to obtain a cashier's check for the full amount he had asked. The routine transaction consumed all of ten minutes.

Mild feelings of remorse were beginning to evolve in Richard's mind as he and the buyer turned to exit. He had owned the 912 longer than he had known his present wife. Which one had received greater cumulative attention was open to speculation.

Richard and the buyer would soon be on their way to the seller's home to secure the title and complete the deal. It is understatement to say that he was waiting anxiously for his last brief turn at the wheel.

As fate dictated, Richard never had the chance for that last drive or even an appreciative goodbye. Wedged in his corner parking spot was a brown Dodge. *His car was gone.* Stolen in less time than it took the teller to type out a check.

Although relieved that he had not yet exchanged his check for the title papers, the buyer was dismayed. For him this car had represented the culmination of several years of searching for a pre-owned Porsche to fully fit his rigid expectations. Richard couldn't help but wonder how his insurance company would figure depreciation.

The 912 was never recovered. The insurance company paid promptly. Richard received a check from his underwriter for only $250 less than he was to have sold it for. Proper compensation was made for valuable accessories and appreciation of the car. Richard retained his holdings only because a seasoned fellow enthusiast had once encouraged him to purchase specially written insurance.

Such good fortune is all too infrequent in the real world of automobile insurance settlements.

Insurance is no less than a documentary instrument with the finality of a *Last Will & Testament* — only with insurance, the owner can be his own beneficiary. Unfortunately the very subject of obtaining insurance coverage of adequate dimension is about as exciting to the average motorist as preparing that Will. It is human nature for the subject to be viewed with mild distrust. For most, even after experience and observation, it remains a great unknown. The necessity for carrying general protection is well understood. (Self-insurance is fine if your name is Rockefeller!) It is also accepted without careful scrutiny as one of the costs of doing the *business of driving.*

Because there is rarely a payoff, it often seems to many that the whole cost is an unjustified expense. After all, odds are against that day of claim. So with hope that the need for settlement will never arise, the subject of coverage is typically dealt with rather summarily in order to dismiss the subject.

Unfortunately, somewhere every hour this common foible leads directly to emotional trauma and substantial personal loss. It need not happen. An understanding of individual policy limitations can effectively curtail such a penalty.

Insurance coverage is a *business* in which every eventuality is spelled out in contractual form. It is also *big* business, for the average company doubles its assets every ten years. Such a record is never achieved by taking in dimes and dishing out quarters. As a business, insurance is plainly written to *win* . . . for the underwriter. Not that it does not provide a necessary service; it does. The fact is, the contract can be written as the owner wants it to read. But unless he so orders, standard forms are applied and protection limits may appear in some devastating areas of coverage after the policy is reviewed for the first time when a claim for a loss is about to be made.

A Porsche owner gambles that nothing will happen when he pays his insurance premium. So does every insured. In contrast, the insurer *never* gambles. The insurance company *knows* what will happen — if not to this insured, then to someone else — and its responsibilities in this scheduled event are neatly fixed beforehand, not surreptitiously but sometimes in retina-wrenching typeface.

Tables derived from case experiences, with previous claims and calculations projecting these findings to the present and future are the foundation on which all insurance premiums are based and policies written. The successful company never deviates from the mean of these findings for a single policy. Underwriting judgments rely almost entirely on statistical evidence which, unfortunately, generally fails to tabulate Porsche performance separately from other "sports" cars. A Fiat Spyder, a TR7, a Datsun 280Z, a Porsche — what's the difference to the company? All are classified together as *sports cars*.

To the average insurer there is little difference. The firm would actually prefer to handle all as one. It seems irrelevant to fiduciary experts that the Porsche owner may well be an exceptional driver and take superior care of his automobile. The insurer is reluctant to accept as fact that the Porsche just happens to be appreciating in value in the midst of a bog of other models which are *depreciating* at one rate or another. It is not of interest to the average insurance company because the concrete evidence to substantiate the theory — driving and loss records of individual owners — has not been spun off as a separate reference table because Porsche owners in class action have not demanded it.

As a Porsche owner, you may ask for and secure individual consideration and treatment from your underwriter. Ask for it by name. It is good practice to contact a well-rooted independent broker or agent and discuss your special requirements. Strive to have him meet them. Most agents have access to a cross-section of companies and will be able to select the best package for your needs.

If the man you are talking with precludes detailed discussion with a "It's all there; *take my word for it,*" he has signaled to you that he *is not* the agent you are seeking to write your special Porsche coverage. *Take no one's word for anything that may be contained in an insurance policy.*

Look for another representative who will give you his ear and then back it up with the footwork to come up with the definitive answers you want. When the policy is presented for acceptance, it should be read and *understood.* Ask questions. The agent will have, or can get, adequate answers to any points you might choose to bring before him relating to coverage. *The man to look for is the representative who drives a Porsche himself.* This agent will speak your tongue.

Staying with a company for an extended period of renewals offers real benefits — particularly when an owner builds up a favorable history pattern, i.e., prompt payments of premiums and few, if any, claims.

Insurance which the average Porsche owner should consider is generally divided into three basic areas of coverage: *comprehensive, collision* and *public liability.*

COMPREHENSIVE

Comprehensive coverage often surfaces with the severest shortcomings. This aspect of protection should compensate the owner for losses incurred by theft, vandalism, fire and esoteric rarities. Although most Porsche owners undoubtedly carry comprehensive insurance, remuneration after a car is stripped, stolen or burned almost always turns out to be less than it should be.

70

This holds especially true for the enthusiast who has done a great deal of work on his Porsche and may have unconsciously transferred his insufficient comprehensive protection from his previous car of a lesser pedigree. The Porsche cannot be adequately protected by insuring it on the same basis as just any car. It is different in a hundred ways, *special*. For one, consider that body work requiring a panel replacement often calls for *leading* the seam between two adjoining panels, a more involved, more skilled task than smearing the cavity with Bondo. Putting a Porsche back together so that market value is retained requires doing the job the way it was originally done. Left to his own devices, the insurer may elect to compensate only for the type of repair that would be acceptable in fixing a Chevette.

An irony — best understood before the fact — is that *insurance terms can mislead* the buyer into feeling comfortable with something less than he may think he is buying. Take, for example, the term *Actual Cash Value*, or *Book Value*. Such a term *sounds good* to the car owner. On analysis, when does a price listing from a cold page take into account the true market value of a Porsche that has been pampered like a jewel?

These terms represent valuations determined on a *depreciated* scale. Assuming that car values usually go down as vehicles age, insurance companies rely on price guides such as the *Kelley Blue Book* or *National Automobile Dealers Association Official Used Car Guide* to determine worth at time of loss. The value for cars older than about seven years isn't even listed in such guides.

When you feel your car is worth more because of exceptional condition, special equipment or desirable vintage or model, you must seek coverage that is designed to compensate according to one of the following terms: *Agreed Value, Stated Amount, Replacement Value,* or *Appraised Value*. Unfortunately, many owners view the cost of such *stated value* coverage as prohibitive. Annual premiums can run as high as 10% to 15% of the value of the car. Current trends in claim settlement, however, indicate that operation of only the most neglected Porsche would not justify the additional cost entailed to implement this type of coverage. Realistically, the problem focuses on finding an underwriter that will accept these terms.

An insurance rate is based on the appraised value of a car, coupled with consideration of the area in which it is operated.

71

Personal garages and less urban localities are among the factors dictating lesser charges. Some companies void coverage when the vehicle is parked on the street. A few underwriters accept a recent bill of sale as an indication of value. Others require a certified appraisal from an authorized Porsche dealer. At least one firm requires that an *approved* anti-theft device be installed prior to the effective date of coverage. It is most beneficial to draw up the papers so the stated value of the Porsche may be *adjusted* — at the owner's option — at any time, to take into account an increase in market value or the addition of new accessories and improvements like mechanical rebuilding or refinishing.

Begin your insurance reprogram by reading your present policy carefully. Do not be mislead by rhetorical clauses. If it distinguishes between the normally equivalent *Book Value* and *Actual Cash Value*, understand the conditions of this stipulation.

If you are compelled to gamble by maintaining a policy indicating settlement on the basis of *Actual Cash Value*, several important precautions should be taken in order to help preserve your equity in the vehicle. Maintain a file of all receipts. Have available letters and appraisals indicating current replacement value. Your mechanic and dealer are good sources for these. Continuously update your file with color photographs to indicate condition. Preserve awards and records of recognition from participation in any *concours* or exhibition in which your car was recognized for its special condition.

In the event of a total loss from theft, you must be prepared to adequately document the condition of the car. A reputable insurance company will seek to settle with a fair adjustment. The figure determined, however, will be contingent upon documentation of the vehicle's true value at time of loss.

Companies commonly hold that any car more than about eight model years' back cannot be worth more than 10% of its original cost. Others may want to hold to a figure in an arbitrary straight line depreciation of, say, 15% per year from date of purchase.

A *Deductible* clause is popularly written into most policies because it makes the amount of the premium easier to accept. The comprehensive program should be reviewed to determine whether there is *Full Coverage* or a major *Deductible* contingency. Does it cover that Leica stolen *from* your car or stolen *with* your car? Or both? Does it provide compensation for renting other wheels in the

72

event of a lay-up or loss?

What are its *Exclusions?* While insurance coverage is rarely written with exclusions so patent that the only sure protection will be to your right front corner, provided it is kicked in by a pregnant zebra running backwards through the Mojave desert at sundown on a Tuesday, *exclusions* do represent the dessert in the insurance feast.

COLLISION

Collision coverage pays for the damage to your car when you cannot collect from another party's insurance company, or when the other driver turns out to be a "turnip," one without insurance or employment.

Insurance adjusters generally rely solely upon special flat-rate manuals when estimating hours of labor needed to replace specific damaged body components on your Porsche. Dependence on these schedules, called "crash books" in the trade, can lead to proposing unrealistic settlements with more trouble to come as a result of the added finesse required for satisfactory reconstruction.

In a revealing article for *Money* magazine, Avery Comarow illuminates some of the problems and offers some valid advice:

> Adjusters tend to regard the [labor] times listed as if the crash books were bibles, but the figures were never intended as gospel. They are computed by auto manufacturers as minimums for warranty work on new cars. The time it takes to remove a rusted-on panel from a five-year-old car and put on a new one will certainly be far longer than for the same work on a car that has been on the road less than a year. Since the time in hours multiplied by the hourly labor rate determines the labor component of the body shop's bill, body shop employees race to beat the manual. That's a race the customer tends to lose; it invites shortcuts, sloppy work and padded bills . . . If the insurance company doesn't at first offer enough money to pay for a good, safe job, bargain with the adjuster. If he refuses to budge, nearly all policies include a valuable but seldom used arbitration clause. It usually calls for you and the company each to hire an independent appraiser — yours can be a body shop — and to split the cost of a third, with the three appraisers determining the size of the settlement. An alternative: have a trustworthy body shop negotiate with the insurer in your behalf.

A heart-rending problem with any damage to your car is that of effectively recovering for the depreciation in the value of the Porsche, suffered above and beyond the repair dollars involved.

The problem becomes tenuous when the claim is made against another party's insurance. Worthy repair and reconstruction work for the Porsche require specially qualified skills and the premium should be set correspondingly higher in order to cover this extra risk. It must be recognized that a section of inner body where structural integrity has been compromised, or even a paint finish bearing tell tales to the trained eye, may depreciate the reconstructed car in excess of repair costs.

If the claims agent makes it clear that settlement for Porsche repair will be handled by his company in the same interest as someone else's Cutlass, it is your signal that the policy will not be sympathetic to your very real problem when and if the day comes when a settlement must be sought.

Precise custom factory jigs are used originally to mate body panels exactly while they are unified into a single body form, whether the car is a Mustang or a Porsche. The difference is in the care and finish rendered during assembly. In the first case, seams are left standing; in the latter each is carefully filled with lead and dressed down so that the whole body appears as a single, sculptured form.

In either case, body shop reconstruction must be performed without reference to the original body jigs. Metal forming is a matter of training and skill. Restoration of a particular surface and contour is up to the eye and the hand of the metal mechanic.

Even in the rare instance where panels are reformed to exacting specifications, Porsche factory paint qualities cannot be duplicated in after-market service. Again, factory conditions are simply not available to the shop, however ideally it may otherwise qualify. A Porsche's original baked finish, once cured at extremely high temperatures, can no longer be subjected to like conditions, except in the rare event in which the body shell is prepared by stripping it of all after assemblies, namely: wiring, upholstery and trim, seals, hardware *et al*. Patch efforts, in spite of common claims, can never achieve precisely the characteristics of the original. Preparation, materials and application techniques, to say nothing of less controlled atmosphere, inevitably result in discrepancies. Most commonly, color matches become disparate to the eye as corrected areas begin to react to light and fair wear at a different rate than the original finish.

74

What happens to a Mustang usually improves it and once back on the road, inadequacies in the repair job are forgotten. What can happen to a Porsche in the same hands might easily do more harm than good. The Mustang may be put back into service at *any* body shop; the Porsche *only where competency prevails.* Going First Class, as in air travel, is going to cost more.

Search and discover the insurance company that is willing to recognize that the Porsche is subject to a market of *discerning* buyers in which a car can currently sell for a number of times its initial market price. This firm will understand what you already know so well: that being compelled to market the car only to the *un*discerning — as the result of having accepted inadequate repair services — is tantamount to deeply depressing its dollar value.

LIABILITY

Liability insurance protects against physical injury and damage claims. It is usually expressed in abbreviated numerical form, such as 15/30/5, with each digit actually a multiple of $1,000. Defined, it means that your insurer places a per accident limit of $15,000 per person for personal injuries, $30,000 for all injuries and $5,000 for property damage. Most states use the numbers cited as a starting point — a minimum requirement.

Today's liberal juries, unfortunately, have regularly awarded judgments ranging into hundreds of thousands of dollars and have brought upright citizens who happened to hold inadequate protection coverage to the depths of financial ruin. Legal experts claim that multiplying each of the numbers above by 10 is not an unrealistic coverage for the Porsche owner to consider.

Driving a Porsche normally causes favorable reaction, if not downright admiration, from the general public. Unfortunately, operating the car can also generate a disparaging response from the self-important critic. The enthusiast finds it easy to ignore this element — except when it finds expression in the jury box. In a court of law, jurors tend to listen when images are painted by the more eloquent of their number of *speeding cars, roaring engines* and *scofflaw driving practices* — images that better characterize the performance of the high school hot-rodder. Most of all, these clerks of life unconsciously tend to hold it against the Porsche owner for his solvency and for his owning and enjoying what they

may deem the premier badge of selfish consumption.

As a result, too often a jury plays Robin Hood and exercises its prerogative to help the have-nots, bringing a whopping verdict against the Porsche owner in any alleged act of negligence. Insurance companies, oblivious to other sensibilities that might negate the wisdom of a rate hike, sometimes take this record into account instead and protect themselves by establishing higher Public Liability rates than are warranted by the proven *lower-than-average* accident frequency among Porsche drivers.

You can get fair insurance provisions for your Porsche, but it takes some conscientious research *before* claim time falls upon you. The reputation a particular company may have already established through its experience with other Porsche owners is worth checking out. A spot survey conducted by questioning, say, ten other owners to determine the parameters of their coverage and to hear something of their personal experiences with their underwriters could turn up a trend, or direct you to a specialist in writing and holding satisfactory protection.

A viable, different approach involves surveying proprietors of several body shops that have come to your attention for their sterling reputation in connection with Porsche rebuilding. These principals will readily disclose particulars of the companies that are willing to settle sufficiently and may also reiterate those that are better avoided, based on recent experience.

It is imperative that you select an underwriter with a reputation for permitting you to have the repairs made by the shop of your choice, using the materials and methods of your choice.

An insurance firm's basic policies are established by its experts on the staff. Ideas are subject to change and refinement as personnel changes occur. So it is important that any facts and figures learned from others' experiences be from the recent past. By the same token any actual listing of cooperative insurance firms cannot be offered here because of continuously changing policies. Yesterday's villain might be today's darling and vise versa.

If you experience difficulty finding an underwriter who will conform to your needs, certain nationally established companies have been commended by the Porsche Club of America for tailoring insurance programs to the real requirements of the owner. Members may write for current information, directing inquiries to Insurance Committee Chairman (Robert R. Gelles, at this writing).

COMPETITIVE DRIVING

No matter how responsively your regular insurance has been written for your needs it will most certainly not cover racing. If you use or plan to use your Porsche competitively, an entirely different and more complex form of protection must be investigated. Coverage for sanctioned events can be outlined by the Porsche Club of America, or by the Porsche Owners Club. Be apprised that coverage for driving in *unsanctioned* events is rarely written.

HELP WHEN IN NEED

The Porsche Club of America established a National Committee called the Valuation Committee in 1979. This group's noble objective is to document and establish values for particular models and years for the purpose of assisting members in alleviating insurance problems that arise from negligent valuations by insurance companies.

Through the use of an established set of references, records are maintained of prices currently being asked for each of the Porsche variations in representative localities throughout the nation. Current value is charted from the most recent six months of data, as may be requested. Value trails drawn from semi-annual price calculations are also used to establish and support long view credibility.

The PCA Valuation Committee findings should not be viewed as a price guideline or an indication for setting a sale asking price. They are intended only to inform a diverse audience of current trends — what the market is bringing. The Club stresses that this service is available only to those members with a legitimate need.

4
OPERATION

The Battle
of the
Boulevard

As David deftly guided his Carrera down a winding approach road to the county airport, a hundred small craft suddenly spread before him in their moorings. His passenger's beaming mood seemed to turn to one of particular sobriety. Charlie was actually sorry to see the destination so quickly that would conclude his first real ride in a Porsche.

It had been usual for him to give David a hard time about the perils of conspicious consumption. Now the skeptic was beginning to realize why one could become so emotionally involved he would invest megabucks in what had until now been dismissed as a "mere automobile, however nicely put together." His own Camaro suddenly struck him as less than adequate.

While the subtleties of Porsche ownership were assimilated in his rider's mind, David nosed his car naturally into a slot next to a sparkling 356 Cabriolet just outside the Beech hanger. Parking beside another Porsche was high in his priorities for reducing cosmetic offenses to the black body.

After inquiring within the hanger, the two associates located the pilot assigned to their special business flight in the act of checking out the aircraft. After a few moments observation, David was impressed by the pilot's thoroughness and quietly marvelled at the clinical manner in which he conducted his inspection.

Nurtured by years of corporate decision-making, David's logical progression of thought and analysis led him to the discovery of a rather enlightening paradox. "I'm beginning to see *why* what we've all heard is true — that statistics indicate passenger miles to be safer by air than by automobile." In his elation he wondered out loud "Why do most motorists neglect monitoring their cars with a similar check list?"

Without a noticeable break in his routine, the pilot smiled and observed, "Laziness primarily. In the first days of motoring it was probably quite different. But today the average driver uses his car like he wears a shoelace — till it breaks. There's a lot of latitude for error without penalty. He knows that he can still coast to a convenient shoulder of the road if there's an electrical or mechanical failure, or if he runs out of fuel. You just don't think that way in an airplane where you have to pay for a mistake. When there isn't any margin for error, it becomes natural to eliminate chances of any error. It's that simple." Then he smiled, "Most cars just don't spark that kind of interest anyway."

"There are some that do," David chanced, speaking for himself.

"Do you mind if I ask what type of car you drive?" the pilot inquired with warming interest.

After David admitted to his respect for his Porsche, the pilot ran his hand over a flap on the left wing in what almost seemed to be a compassionate gesture. "To be honest, I've been giving my old 356 the full inspection longer than I've had a license to fly."

David indulged the 45 minute flight in sharing experiences with the pilot, while Charlie fingered the lock on the attache case in his lap and wondered what the two up front would think if they could see his unkempt Camaro.

INSPECTION

Every pilot conducts a routine inspection of his craft prior to every flight. Precautions and back-up procedures suggested by the Federal Aviation Administration have become the way of life in flying. As a result passenger miles by air travel are safer than by automobile, as David had read. If statistics show, as they do, that there are actually fewer deaths per hundred thousand passenger miles by air than by highway, the flight procedure approach to Porsche operation is a worthy proposal.

In the fine line, your Porsche may be singularly different every day; variables abound. Are wheels balanced perfectly at speed? Is tire wear commensurate with the tread? Are tire pressures adequately monitored?

But in addition to tire checks, trailing arms may feel loose, excessive oil may exist below the engine at some particular drop point. That Turbo you played loosing tag with on the freeway may have increased the wear on your brake pads. When there is any question, check it or have it checked. For the true Porsche enthusiast, *man and machine are one.*

It's an unfortunate commentary that the average American car owner is not as maintenance conscious as his counterpart abroad. This disparity makes it tough on image for the foreign product that was not engineered to bear up blindly under neglect.

A special few other imported automobiles have been so well engineered — the Porsche is paramount in this group — that lax servicing would be tantamount to a sin. "When you don't change the oil in the aluminum engine of a Porsche," observed Pontiac general manager Robert Stempel, "then people think you're a bad driver. But if you were to burn up the aluminum engine in a Chevrolet because you didn't change the oil, you would say that GM did it to you. An iron engine can take abuse." So it is that much car design for the mass consumer has been planned to protect the driver from himself.

The Porsche owner must often take into account the general consumer's lack of compassion for his car. To avoid *certain grief* sooner or later, the only stance to assume at your corner service station is one of viewing the facility more as a *dis*service station.

The price of permitting the average gashouse jockey to "serve" is too great. Chipped finish around the fuel filler door and a hand-sanded outer windshield surface are guaranteed by-products over a period of time. [Illustrated page 82] Have you ever seen an attendant approach your windshield with a clean rag? There seems to be a charm associated with using the same cloth in the same grey-watered bucket without end. That rag can carry more grit than an application of Duco 7.

This should serve as a continuous reminder that the chores usually performed by the attendant, from filling the fuel tank to checking the oil and cleaning the windshield, are chores the owner must perform for himself.

Dimensions in inspection should tap greater depths than the purely visual. To the believer, his Porsche develops its own special set of exclusive characteristics in handling and aging, and communication of a changing condition can be immediate. The owner's ears and nose, as well as his eyes, should be called upon to detect problems before they lead to major damages. Every noise and odor has its implications. As with learning a foreign language, you can trace origins and determine meaning if you know a few basics.

Many mechanical failures are transmitted as audible sounds on the road. Their messages can be very revealing. Sensitivity and the cultivation of an ear for translation will enable you to distinguish the inherent from the irregular. When your car is in for its regular service, be prepared to communicate with the mechanics as to aberrations that may exist. As an elementary guide in identifying the more common special sounds, the following list is offered:

Buzzing: defective speedometer or tachometer cable
Groaning: loose wheel bearings, backing plates or brake drums
Growling: worn clutch, transmission or driveshaft
Hissing: loose spark plug or disengaged vacuum hose
Humming: worn rear axle
Knocking: burned out main bearings, connecting rods or piston pins
Pinging: lean mixture, improper octane fuel or excessive spark advance
Popping: thermal expansion of plastic instrument lenses
Rapping: low oil pressure or worn main bearings
Rattling: loose muffler, detachable top parts, suspension, window lift mechanism
Scraping: worn brake lining
Screeching: out-of-round brake drums or loose brake shoe lining
Snapping: cracked distributor cap, broken or loose spark plug wires
Squealing: slipping belt, bad generator, exhausted brake pads
Tapping: maladjusted valve tappets
Thumping: Out-of-balance tires, overinflated tires, poor front-end alignment, bent driveshaft, worn universal joint
Whining: Worn brake shoes, generator bearings, wheel bearings or loose fan belt

Identifying unaccustomed odors can be beneficial. For example, the smell of burning rubber — when you haven't mischievously popped the clutch — usually indicates heated wire insulation and a probable electrical short circuit. A sweet, pungent, paint-remover type scent hints at leaky brake cylinders. The permeating essence of gasoline more obviously indicates deterioration at some point in the fuel line.

An effective measure in preventive maintenance can be a quarterly *test run* carried out in a similar fashion to the "case history" kept on a boat by the avid mariner. Regardless of frequency of use, try prescribing one "cruise" periodically solely as a "physical" for the purpose of noting potential defects, necessary repairs and possible improvements. These factors should be observed and noted *while testing* the vehicle, rather than after the testing, when it may not be possible to recall every item vividly. A tape recorder serves best, with entries made in the random form of running commentary.

Once noted, you may choose to correct inconsistencies immediately, but more important, you have become aware of the current limitations in your car. This pertinent worklist may be kept in the glove compartment for reference with updating entries added as you correct the points listed on a regular program.

Practice knowing yourself as well as the Porsche. Remember the hand in the glove syndrome in which car and driver act as one. An awareness of some basics will enable you to dovetail effectively in a given situation. Reaction times are as potentially disparate as the circumstances you are likely to encounter in driving. If ever compelled to drive while ill, proceed at no more than three-quarter speed to allow for reaction time that surely would prove greater. Driving under the influence of any substance, even tobacco, has been known to alter general perceptions measurably. Your mental state is as important as your physical well being. Anger can produce irrational response in a tight situation. Fatigue, permitted to advance without acknowledgement, can lead to hazardous straits.

Audit overall alertness periodically as you drive at night. Consider the eye strain inherent in driving after dark. Approaching sets of headlights are relatively dim at first. Then they make the near approach and fade in passing in what amounts to a quick bright flash. Ophthalmologists claim that the eye can readily accommodate to the flash, but is reluctant in adapting back to the ensuing darkness. Constant readjustment to these extremes causes eye muscles to tire. Allow for this. Some drivers close their eyes for the instant of this last flood of light before a car passes, thus avoiding extreme dilating of the pupils.

DRIVING

Thoughts on the real nature of being underway in an automobile were expressed nicely in *The Safe Driving Handbook,* a compilation by the Aerospace Education Foundation.

The main thing about your environment is that you are traveling in a fixed roadway on the surface of the earth. As you move, there is constant change, but you have only so much leeway in which to maneuver. You have to deal with the conditions which appear on the roadway. That is the big difference in freedom between you and the pilot of a plane or the captain of a ship. Every change in the weather affects you and the car; there is no way for you to gain altitude and get away from the weather. You have no radar and no two-way radio to weatherman and air controllers, so you are, in effect, going solo, and you are therefore affected in a major way by any change to twilight or to darkness. You still have to stick to that stretch of road, rain or shine, light or dark, if you're going to get somewhere.

Then there is that all-important fact: the traffic. You in your car are still part of society. In fact, you are in something which is a very special social system all by itself. Traffic is a social situation. Unlike most other groups, a traffic group is composed of strangers who are interacting with each other. Nearly everyone goes to some form of this social affair every day. We consider it quite ordinary, but never in all history has there been a social system quite like it.

Traffic is something like a parade — there are people in the streets and there are people watching. Traffic certainly is like a battle, because the dead and wounded compare in number with America's war casualties.

Traffic is almost universal in America, and in many ways it is quite democratic; there is a certain right to the road that anyone can share if his car will drive onto the roadway. The right to move freely from one place to another is to most Americans a deeply cherished freedom.

At the same time, traffic is often called a punishment. Yet again it seems that at times people play it as a game. As a social game it is not private but public — you go every day and still can't choose your company. You have to play with whoever shows up.

It is good to consciously apply the first few stops and turns of the day as a testing period to evaluate the response of driver and car — and car and driver — so you can coordinate efforts against negative forces that may be indicated. Program your memory with pertinent notes. What you discover and register when no external pressure is present may be recalled to mind in that emergency when a split second counts and you have literally no time to think.

For the sporting Porsche driver, it is often scenic back country travel that offers the most pleasurable road work. Around demanding curves, over a lush rise to an obscure straightaway an enamored driver tends to ignore his formal speed readings and their inherent limitations. Unfortunately, coroner reports generally confirm that just such beautiful remote roads are a primary scene for the head-on collision.

Most fatal errors on the road can be traced to inadequately determining stopping distance. Road surface is always a critical factor. Well maintained concrete provides the optimum traction. In order of declining retention, asphalt, tar, stabilized dirt, gravel and loose dirt must be considered.

You must always account for *speed and distance* as well as surface geography. Awareness of specific braking capabilities is as important to the driver as relative altitude is to the pilot. Neither should have to rely on a seat-of-the-pants feeling. Just as radar gives the pilot a reading on his distance from other objects, the speedometer in your Porsche may be used to compute how far you are from other cars or obstacles. Dry run panic stopping is not in anybody's book beyond the manufacturer's test grounds. *It is too hard on both car and driver.*

Consequently the average driver cannot build a history of experience in this area. The law of inertia spells out that a moving object tends to continue moving and not even the most elaborately equipped competition car can be constructed to stop on the proverbial "dime". Assuming ideal terrain and discounting reaction time, the average Porsche will consume almost the length of a football field before coming to a complete stop from a speed of only 60 mph. The distance can be shortened somewhat by forcing abuse upon tires and suspension. Even with the finest radials and suspension elements a wet surface would more than double stopping distance.

Never hesitate to switch on your headlights when driving in dim or diffused light. At dawn or dusk an unreflective road sign or even a pedestrian may recede into the flat and shadowy landscape. Glare can be decreased and overall vision extended by cleaning a dirty windshield just before entering the twilight zone.

Cultivate the capacity for correlating road signs and assimilating natural indications and physical obstructions to compile a readout that will enable you to be a master under the infinite variables of the road. Remember that your car's reaction time and response is limited by your own. Successful driving through the uncertainties of strange territory is contingent on many factors.

An accomplished motorist makes mental notes periodically of the breadth and composition of the road before him. Standard lanes are twelve feet in width. The average car measures six feet, leaving three feet on each side. Rural roads commonly have lanes only ten feet wide. Some existing roads are only eight feet across, or less.

One of Germany's most prominent rally drivers and Porsche enthusiasts, Walter Röhrl, claims that successful competition drivers can enlighten the public to another critical factor of total automobile control, that of effectively judging the terrain on first approach.

"The competition driver develops a special acuity through observation of road patterns, fencing and telephone line installations that forewarn of dips and other surface changes in order to make as much of a known quantity out of a given situation as such clues permit."

Why does a chicken cross the road?

Perhaps to indicate to you that you may find a cow in front of your Porsche just around the next bend.

Studies show that about 90% of the information relevant to traffic conditions potentially assimilated by a driver is perceived *visually.* Consequently, the successful operator must train his eyes accordingly. In his book *Revolution Am Steuer – Die Neue Fahrtechnik,* Finnish competition driver Ruano Aaltonen cites the following list of sight guidelines, composed originally by the German government agency that conducts compulsory inspections of all automobiles every two years, as being essential for the conscientious sports car driver:

On open stretches of highway–

The farther ahead you look, the easier it is to stay on course, to find and hold your lane.

Avoid "zeroing in" unnecessarily on things or events.

Keep the eyes free to move and adapt, even when there seems to be nothing of importance going on and you believe it is safe to divert your attention momentarily from driving.

If an obstruction suddenly appears ahead, don't freeze your eyes on it; for example, if traffic grinds to a halt and you are moving along at a good clip, instead of staring at the brake lights ahead look for a way out of or around the jam.

In curves –
Direct your view mainly to the inner boundaries of your own lane.
When "threading the needle" –
Narrow passages can be negotiated more steadily and with more certainty if the view is directed to the middle of the passage.

Aaltonen adds that "Practiced drivers scan left, right and center when negotiating lefthand curves and concentrate on the right side when turning right."

A Porsche is built to be driven harder than many other cars. But the Porsche should never be subjected to undue abuse simply *because* it was engineered to take it, even though experts declare it cannot be *overdriven.*

Running at red-line engine speeds is not sound procedure. Some drivers feel that towering rpm and short bursts of second gear between traffic signals help to "clean out" a Porsche engine. Irrational heating and cooling of the combustion chamber may not only destroy spark plugs but can be instrumental in breaking down bearings, timing chains, valve guides, piston rings and cylinder walls.

This is not to say that air-cooled Porsche engines run well in the low end of 2000 rpm where sufficient cooling air is not provided for a sustained engine load. However, attaining 5000 rpm in second cannot be used to super-cool and "save" your engine. Most Porsches can be happy at 2600 to 3000 rpm during sustained speeds on level terrain. Gradual deceleration from such a run without downshifting will also minimize wear. While brake pads are far more expendable than transmissions, the universal practice of braking for intersections, rather than downshifting as a matter of greater control, is understandably unpopular with many Porsche drivers.

One recalls Denis Jenkinson's observation that originally appeared in the British *Motor Sport:*

"You can drive a Porsche as hard as you like and you will not run out of roadholding or stability; in fact you can drive it as hard as it will go without any qualms, for it not only feels stable at all times, but is stable. If you drive a 4.2 E-Type Jaguar as hard as it will go, you will have a very big accident."

Stop-and-go driving patterns in traffic are largely provoked by the myopic driver. Observing farther ahead, to determine whether you are approaching a light in the first part or the latter part of its time period before change, will enable you to move smoothly through more green lights than ever.

Driving ahead of your car can take even more sophisticated form than anticipating signals. If you foresee upcoming circumstances by changing to lower gears when the need for a short burst of power will be required by a given situation, you can safely run at 2800 rpm all day long. As in playing the simple signal game, the name of the skill is *anticipation*. This superior driving technique in the hands of many Porsche drivers fosters the legend that the car can be safer "than just any car" because of its innate controllability at speed. Accidents have been avoided by literally driving *around* sudden hazards.

The skill recognizes that the key to avoiding contact with other vehicles is to *expect the unexpected* and *prepare for it as though it were inevitable*. Reflex times are shaved by this advance thinking. Primary in developing driving foresight is cultivation of an instinct for monitoring variables of terrain and weather, of other traffic and light sources, and of assessing their potential for altering handling values.

By continuous consideration of *What if?* the expert steadily translates these running conditions into emergency options in relation to his Porsche's best interests.

As the miles tick by, favorable escape routes from the roadway may be sought and assessed. Would that terrain serve as a deceleration ramp if brakes were to fail right now in this downhill hairpin? Is this shoulder negotiable at speed, or will it flip the car to slip into it with only the right side wheels? Can I go into a controlled roll safely at this point if a head-on collision could not be averted otherwise? Or over there? Etc. Anticipation — the *if* factor — presents a challenging discipline to the serious driver.

BAD WEATHER CONTROL: RAIN, SNOW, ICE

Rain does not have to be heavy for a slippery surface to conquer your vehicle. Light drizzle can spew even the best handling car into the center median. The early minutes or even first few seconds of a rain storm, as the soot and oils on the pavement are transformed into an almost soapy mixture, can be among the most treacherous. Attempting a quick stop on a freshly dampened surface may prove as ineffective as on oil-slicked cement. Controlled handling to slow down before *hydroplaning* occurs is all important.

This hazardous force that compounds with increased speed — the actual lifting of the tire off the road surface by a thin layer of water under the tread — is a phenomenon that reduces effective friction to the point that directional control becomes lost and the car begins to drift into a spin. As the hydrostatic reaction occurs forward of the axle centerline on your Porsche, sustained hydroplaning will tend to void front tire rotation.

To regain control in the event your Porsche's front end does in fact succumb to hydroplaning: take your foot off the accelerator; do not touch the brakes; do not turn the wheel however slightly. As speed is reduced, your tires will slice through the layer of water beneath and you will then be able to assume control.

If you simply remember the essential elements of wet weather control, hydroplaning can be avoided and your Porsche's superior tracking ability can be felt. Inertia and centrifigal force must be respected more than ever. Reduce speed — less than 50 mph is appropriate when you suspect water to be ⅛ inch or more in depth. (In hard rain, water depth is likely to be greater in the right lane; try to follow the crown.) Negotiate corners at half the speed of usual capability. Allow more than the recommended safe margin between you and the car ahead. Make no sudden moves in steering or braking. Periodically pump the brakes. Keep headlights on and clean for optimum visibility during a downpour.

Contrary to wishful thinking, Mother Nature can turn the tables even on a Porsche. In wet weather driving it is fallacy to rest with the idea that it takes two to Tango. Wise was the driver who first observed "Being the best driver in the country doesn't impart an immunity from becoming involved from a lesser driver's error."

Develop an acuity for "reading" clues on the road that convey the driving aptitude of those around you. Whenever you detect evidence of the inept, react by increasing the space between your car and the novice.

Many marginal drivers initiate moves *before* signaling. When overtaking a slower driver, a well-timed glance at his left front tire may indicate an intention of changing lanes or turning even as the offending operator is first becoming conscious of what he is doing.

In Washington D.C., in a scientific study of driving, researchers took motion pictures of 304 cars as they went through city traffic. It was found that 87 percent of these drivers went over the speed limit, 17 percent followed too closely, 46 percent turned without signaling, 15 percent rushed a traffic light, and 34 percent stopped improperly. These 304 drivers averaged nine errors each. (From *The Safe Driving Handbook*)

When driving in icy winter conditions, look for surfaces that promote good adhesion. On ice and snow so much traction is lost that the car's stopping distance may be increased by as much as twelve times. Be alert to melted patches, grit and roughness and try to manage serious braking and accelerating selectively on these areas of the roadway. Skid correction is well defined and is an infinite topic in itself. Most agree that the best way to control a skid is to avoid it in the first place. Sudden movements of the steering wheel or unwarranted braking will thrust even a Porsche into a side slip. When a skid begins to occur, the natural impulse to steer the Porsche out of the skid is correct. Under-correction is critical; be certain not to overcompensate. Over-correction may bring about a very common highway accident, the non-collision upset. Although a skid can be provoked by a driver's cornering too fast, it is more often the byproduct of harsh braking. For the skilled driver it is reassuring just how efficiently a Porsche steers in an emergency *without* braking. Fortunately through the years the Porsche *aficionado* has been generally more adept behind the wheel than most drivers, otherwise the threat of extinction would be hanging heavy over early models today.

Light snow contributes many of the effects of rain with the extra hazard of rutting that could provide the driver with the over-riding feeling that he is on automatic pilot. Unfamiliar roads require special caution. Again, be particularly aware of other drivers nearby and try to anticipate any particular failings.

Under all adverse conditions it is essential to keep moving and make yourself visible to others — *always*. In dense fog, movement can be the difference for survival. Be alert to the problems other drivers may be facing in their less roadable cars.

Inclement weather operation is punishing to the vehicle. The surest formula for these days is to leave the Porsche safely housed, preserving it for more favorable occasions when you can appreciate fully the finer points of its handling characteristics. Bad

weather days make owning that second "go-for" car especially worthwhile.

PARKING: CATCHING PORSCHE PARANOIA

Porsche driving leads to the study of parking as a fine art. It is immediately evident that *driving is safer for the car than parking*. In motion you can usually choose to provide space away from other vehicles as you elect. When left at rest, it is too much to hope that others will respectfully avoid opening their doors against your body panels. Diagonal parking between a pick-up truck and a ten-year-old Lincoln courts *certain* disaster. Except when you can become the middle Porsche, it is best to avoid diagonal parking altogether.

To preserve your car's original form it is necessary to totally avoid common situations. Average drivers never worry about those necessary occasions when they must leave their cars unattended in public streets or parking lots. Everyone is aware of the unnerving toll taken by mishandled shopping carts in shopping center parking areas. How does one win at this costly game?

Most Porsche people instinctively straddle a line to consume two spaces so there is a broad margin on either side of the car. This will only produce the desired protection *if* other drivers respectfully observe the painted line spaces around you. Another reflex action in parking leads the Porsche to a space between vehicles of similar status or position. Often a space can be found next to a planter, near protective poles, or even amidst some trees or other available stationary objects where the car will not become the literal butt of others' inept car jockeying. [Illustrated page 92]

When compelled to park regularly in an area with other automobiles, first commandeer the spot safest from back-stopping. Then, if you own the building, set off your special parking space with iron pipe railings (the type like school and industry stairwell railings), preferably so positioned that the average full-sized car would find it difficult to swing into your place anyhow. If you don't own the building, take this initiative on a Sunday morning anyhow. Prebuilt running lengths of this type of assembly can commonly be purchased from the larger house-wrecking firms. Otherwise, fabrication from scratch still represents an elementary exercise worth every moment it might demand. [Illustrated page 92]

How much thought do you give to the places you choose to park before the fact? Do you weigh the pros and cons of a potential spot? Your chosen car, unfortunately, has been known to act as a magnet in attracting mishaps. A sixth sense can guide the Porsche owner away from a lot of grief if he knows what to train himself to observe.

The periphery of a building under construction or one undergoing a repainting should be recognized as a fall-out zone. There are other hazards less obvious. Ever look up at a telephone pole and visualize a pair of channel lock pliers seeking freedom from a repairman's tool belt and hitting the top of your car with considerable velocity? Ever wonder why the golfer at the country club seeks refuge for his Porsche at the opposite end of the layout from the driving range? Have you considered just how foul afield some of those baseballs are struck by Little League stars? Would you really park *en masse* at a fairgrounds?

A simple weekly visit to your dry cleaning shop could lead to complications. The steam and solvents that spew out of exhaust vents in a wall of such establishments should be carefully observed before parking. Consider all that foot traffic includes people getting in and out of their cars with wire coat hangers in tow. The extra walk from parking clear of such potential hazards — and it's healthy too — is the most common measure you can take to increase odds in your Porsche's favor.

Bob Hope once reported that he parked so far away from the Rose Bowl for the New Year's Day football game to protect his new car from others that he walked by his own house on the way to the field. Parking in a protected or remote area in order to preserve your Porsche should not involve quite this hardship.

Practice observing general parking accommodations in the place you must use before tying up to the hitching rack. Consider conditions that have the potential to bruise your car and strive to avoid them. Not every shadow of doubt will lead to negative results. But objectively noting conditions as they exist surely will pay off in fewer body scars.

While both parallel and diagonal parking should ideally be ruled out, occasions arise when even the Porsche must be compelled to meld with existing public parking. When required to park in a congested area or between other vehicles, the use of side moldings

94

might be considered as supplementary protection. These add-ons perform essentially the purpose of rub strips while getting low marks for aesthetics. Only the Speedster was so fitted at the factory. The permanent installation may only be considered when a car might be forced to a concentrated diet of this kind of parking.

Temporary rub strips should be considered. Some are magnetic-backed neoprene pads, others clip to door edges or wrap into the closed door well. [Illustrated page 96]

Positioning the Porsche so it will be least likely to incur contact from a vehicle moving in reverse gear is worthy of prime consideration each time out. It is unfortunate that so many everyday motorists in large American cars (with and without trailer hitches) only change direction in parallel parking maneuvers after making contact with the car parked behind. [Illustrated page 97] Don't permit your Porsche to be there.

Bumpers and related override bars play an important part in the protection of both sides of the car in every scene populated by other automobiles. Some accessory manufacturers produce tubular add-ons that extend the protection provided by the original bumpers in construction design that does not detract from the car's stock character. [Illustrated page 98]

Unless you happen to occupy a private world in which no other cars are at large, removal of the original bumpers — presumably in cult worship of cosmetic purity — is most unrealistic and foolhardy. [Illustrated page 99]

Ever try thinking like a thief? This mental exercise could save your car. What does the thief think when he locates a desirable Porsche in the extended parking area of an airport storage yard? To him the Porsche resting in the parking lot of a theater might as well have a neon sign in the window blinking "Back in not less than two hours. Help yourself to all or part!"

Thinking ahead where you are going to have to "light" is part of the art that becomes a science when you must continue to use the same public thoroughfares and facilities all others use — and there is no other way.

Police records profile the most enticing spot for Porsche theft as the top of a hill on a dark street. When parking at the curb try to locate where traffic or pedestrian travel is active. *Choose an illuminated spot.* The thief tends to be wary of pedestrian pas-

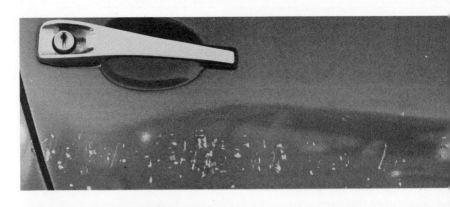

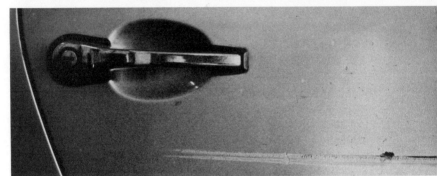

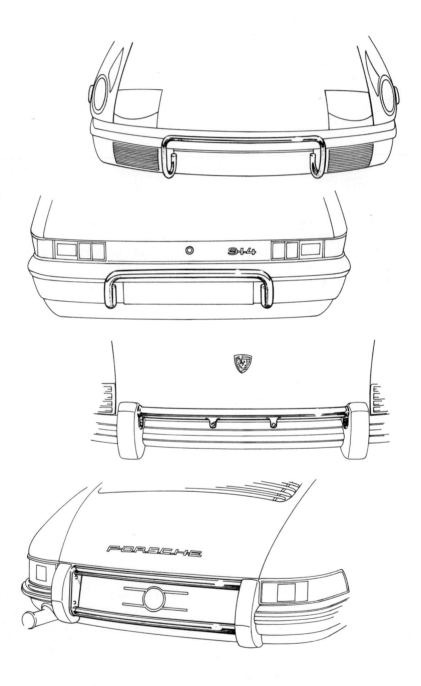

sersby because anyone approaching on foot could materialize as the owner.

Instances have been documented in which the thief waited for his victim to approach him on "home turf." The urban parking lot generally is a popular target area. Many big city facilities even aid the thief, unwittingly, by requiring that keys be left with the car. Attendants have even been known to joy ride with cars left in their care.

In that rare event in which you must conform to the key-with-the-car demand, it is wise to keep a scratch pad handy. In conspicious view of the attendant you might enter the car's odometer reading and fuel gauge level prior to handing over the key. It is wise to be evasive and foreshortening in any necessary conversation with the attendant in indicating the time of your absence from the lot. On return, a 360 degree visual check should be made to see that all is intact before claiming your car.

Specialists in Porsche theft have often become professional in their operations to a withering degree. Experienced thieves have been known to employ spotters capable of intense surveillance of you and your Porsche. These "bird dogs" report where you work, where you play, wherever you take your automobile on a regular basis and document it all with a stopwatch.

Reportedly in the thief's view, the easiest snatch is said to occur around eight or nine in the evening while the general public is preoccupied and trusting. Thieves recognize that after midnight the public tends to become more suspicious.

Nearly 60 percent of stolen Porsches are lifted from private homes, apartment garages and residential streets. Commercial areas account for another 30 percent. Statistically, car theft is an urban dilemma and, correspondingly, the more concentrated the urban area, the more intensive the problem. New York City, to cite an example, was the scene of somewhat more than 100,000 vehicle thefts during 1979.

There are many sites where the Porsche is more plainly vulnerable. By assessing your regular personal itinerary you can pinpoint what may be particularly unprotected spots. Regard even innocent-appearing changes with suspicion.

One former owner of a 356C who had treasured his car since 1964 failed to question a minor discrepancy near his regular daily parking place. As a result he had to accept his insurance settlement and the car was never recovered. On his last day with the car, he observed that the concrete pre-cast barrier, placed as a front wheel stop to prevent rolling slightly downgrade into an adjacent property's parking lot, was missing. Not giving this a second thought was to prove a fatal error — as he would discover when he stepped out of the building that afternoon to drive home.

The curb had been removed for a very special reason: in its absence it became a swift, silent move to ease the 356 forward into the lower lot unobserved and then spirit it away. The two-stage theft was necessary because the thieves, having done their homework, knew that if the car were moved backward they would have been seen by anyone who happened to look out of the rear of the building.

An equally aggressive scheme recently surfaced in a small west coast college town. Heart-of-gold Vicki returned to her apartment in her green Targa from an evening class at the university to discover her garage door padlocked with an alien unit.

Puzzled by being summarily locked out, but fatigued from a pressing night of examinations, she was not inclined to look for a dark motive in the unexplained switch. Instead, she began to turn over in her mind just which of her many acquaintances had been the prankster who had engineered this gentle inconvenience. Seeking an expedient solution, she simply slipped the 911 into an available slot in a dark side street around the corner and headed back to her place on foot, determining to find someone with bolt-cutters early the next morning.

When the sun came up Vicki found that it was not boltcutters that she needed but an automobile. Her parking decision of a few hours earlier had been choreographed for her by a creative crew of auto rustlers.

STORAGE

Porsches living amidst the four seasons are often stored for the winter. In some cases a driver may have such priorities that a particular vehicle figures only in very limited use. (Perhaps he owns six vintage Porsches and is fulfilling a plan to drive each in rotation!) An automobile that is laid up part of the time is likely to deteriorate more rapidly than in regular use if proper care is not observed. The following recommendations apply to a Porsche that is to be laid up for a winter or more:

1. Clean interior and exterior thoroughly.
2. Fill fuel tank.
3. Fill tires to 50 psi (unless manufacturer's precautionary warning indicates otherwise).
4. Drain oil from a warm crankcase.
5. Change filter and refill with a *preservative* oil.
6. Run engine to normal oil temperature to circulate the new lubricant.
7. Disconnect fuel line and attach a short piece of durable flex hose to the carburetor. Place hose in kerosene and run the engine for 30 seconds or until it stops, whichever comes first.
8. Reconnect fuel line, wiping up any spilled kerosene.
9. Cap the tail pipe with duct tape.
10. Disconnect positive cable at battery.
11. Spray discs or brake drums with a "mechanic's helper."
12. Lift wiper arms away from windshield.
13. Disengage clutch by depressing pedal. Use a short section of wood placed snugly between dashboard and pedal to hold it down.

To restore the car to service:

a. Drain carburetor and fuel line of kerosene.
b. Deflate tires to recommended psi.
c. Reconnect battery.
d. Drain crankcase and replace with the proper motor oil.
e. Restore wiper arms against windshield.
f. Release pedal to re-engage clutch.
g. Turn engine by hand to check for correct operation.
h. Prime the carburetor and start.

Ideally, the Porsche should be operated periodically even during short periods of disuse. If the steps outlined are not taken, it is essential that the car be run once every two weeks or so till normal operating temperature is attained. If it is not feasible to drive it, 2000 rpm is sufficient for standing warm-up.

Disuse practically mandates some mortality within the hydraulic brake system. Conventional brake fluids tend to accumulate substantial condensation. Hydroscopic moisture, the formal term for this condition, precipitates deterioration of seals and engenders corrosion.

Silicone type brake fluid, which is anti-hydroscopic in composition, should be used when a car must be stored often or is not being driven on a daily basis. The system must be thoroughly flushed and bled to change over, preferably by a professional. This measure may involve expense and inconvenience but will successfully halt further deterioration in the hydraulic system.

If your Porsche is to be stored unstarted for 90 days or more, you may want to perform the following tasks in addition to those previously listed.

1. Remove spark plugs.
2. Spray preservative oil into the cylinders.
3. Replace spark plugs.
4. Wipe the head and exhaust pipes with oil before plugging tail pipe.
5. Spray the underside of the engine with an oil film.

Although effective in preserving the mechanics of your car during long periods of inactivity, these additional procedures are regarded as unnecessary by many who regularly store one or more automobiles for extended periods. The superior alternative to dead storage is always to start the car periodically to cook out condensation build-up.

Safe storage is only possible in a clean, dry area. Consider covering with a light Polycotton (breathable) covering as soon after exterior cleaning as possible.

CAR COVERS

An extensive variety of individual cover designs fall within three primary formats. The tonneau cover, the gravel shield, and the complete cover. The first type is of interest only to the owner of a car with a completely removable top like a Speedster or Spyder.

The gravel shield, commonly called a "bra," is effective in preventing a frontal onslaught — damaging to finish and glass — from the slush of the roadbed. [Illustrated page 106] Like its namesake, the bra comes in an array of styles and shapes. [Illustrated pages 104-105]

A working version, which German technicians refer to as a *Steinschlagschutzhulle,* is used during pre-shipment testing at the factory.

Owner emotions run the gamut as to the appearance of this type of protector. Some drivers tolerate it without comment; others swear it detracts. There are also those who choose to leave a bra in place as much as possible, thinking of it as a "sporty" style note. This group may have an ulterior reason for doing this.

106

Actually, use of the bra gravel guard requires care. The car and the bra must be clean and dry before they are mated. Even so, after a period of time this protector may scratch fenders as a result of friction caused by the wind-pumping between the material and the car's finish. Any impurities that exist between tend to act like so much grinding compound. So it is that the owner with that bra in place on his car too much of the time actually may be using it to conceal abrasion marks.

A gravel shield must be removed and thoroughly dried if it has become wet. If permitted to remain in place wet after the sun romes out it can cause discoloration and other paint mutations, the result of trapped moisture and reaction to heat.

Bras are fabricated to conform to the fenders and lay flush on the nose, or are fitted to stretch taut from fender to fender. Some are designed to cover the hood area only. The latter styles reportedly offer the greatest protection from highflying debris. When ordering a bra, it is necessary to consider any auxiliary elements such as fog lamps that may be mounted at the front of the car. Specific information as to the location and size of spoilers, nerf bars, bumper guards and license plate mountings must be furnished for successful custom fitting. If a bra is fitted with holes cut for accessories that the car does not carry, the unit will be prone to excessive fluttering and flapping at speed. If accommodation is not provided for add-ons, use of these accessories will be forfeited while the bra is in position and its extremely tight stretch fit may contribute to other problems.

A functional, but aesthetically wanting, alternative to the bra is the Plexiglas shield designed to mount in front of the bumper as a great wall. This simple device intercepts stones and insects and does not trap moisture. Wind resistance may be increased to a certain degree and appearance is not enhanced, but when one accepts its function these shortcomings become insignificant. The shield has been used most often for long distance or cross-country travel protection.

The total car cover envelopes the entire form while it is at rest. [Illustrated page 108] Minimizing moisture collection in this type of protection presents an unending struggle. This cover does not provide worthy protection in a rain storm but serves to obscure from the direct sunlight and keep dust from nesting. A fully co-

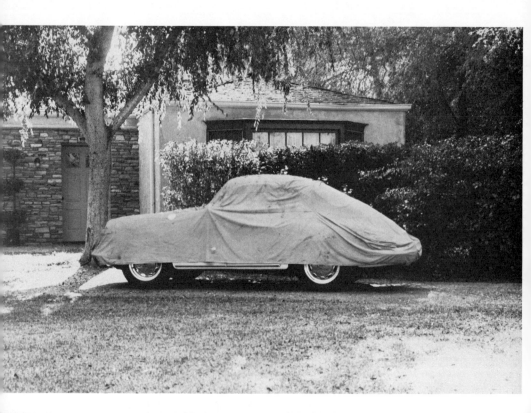

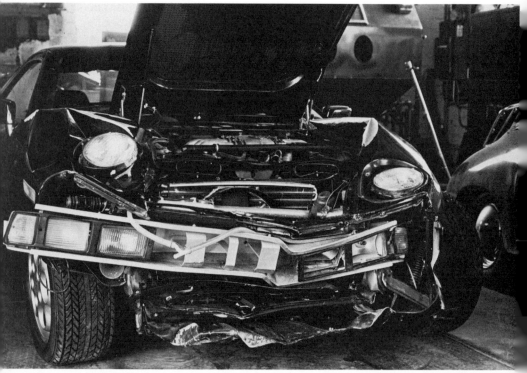

vered car, housed in a garage, will be protected from abrasions and its finish will be kept cleaner longer. The full cover offers the added feature of keeping the interior moderately protected and away from the public eye.

Paint experts have claimed that if a car is subjected to even two hours a day of stationary exposure to sun and dirt, use of a cover could be worthwhile. Sunlight and dirt begin on Day One to take their toll in paint finish, chromium plating, rubber parts, leather and vinyl. Premature aging that requires replacement of any of these materials on the Porsche can easily exceed the initial cost of the cover. When to cover and when not to cover should be governed by common sense rather than by fetish.

Without protection, chemicals in the atmosphere, as well as dirt and other abrasive matter air borne by passing cars, will tend to settle in and about your Porsche. As a result, the finish and interior become unnecessarily susceptible to deterioration. The sun's rays — the most underrated natural bleaching action known — can make even the most lavish paint finish fugitive. Light-colored covers reflect more rays and are less apt to retain heat.

In a persistent wind or in wet weather it is better to leave the car uncovered. While a cover is difficult to handle in the wind, on a relatively calm day it can be folded expediently by an individual.

The full cover is an aid in keeping your car clean between washings, preventing paint oxidation and discouraging tampering. Colors, materials and prices vary. The cheapest and least effective type is constructed of clear polyethylene plastic. The most desirable is double-stitched, elastic band fitted, cable locked to the car and tailored from a light-colored poly/cotton machine washable material. Flannel covers are recommended only for long-term storage in a dry environment. Should you use a cover in lieu of a garage, a *porous* fabric must be used to prevent the adverse effects that begin with night condensation and generate mildew action.

There is, of course, obvious reason *never* to cover a hot exhaust with any cover.

There are relocatable shelters on the market that will simulate garage protection in frequented spots away from home base. Initial expense and difficulty in transporting have generally acted to negate their casual use.

TOWING THE PORSCHE

Bumper attachment for towing should be as off limits to the Porsche owner as permitting a shop cloth to be picked up off the floor and used to wipe the windshield. The mortality rate from inept towing of the Porsche has been a serious factor over the years. The majority of towing damages have resulted not from owners' makeshift arrangements but from misapplications and other poor judgments on the part of towing personnel using commercial practices.

Though unlikely, if you are ever detained for excessive speed and incarceration appears inevitable, avoid towing if within your command. Insist on another licensed driver of *your choosing* being permitted to drive the car in lieu of the wrecker service. (If you are taking the Speedster on a run to check out new jets, better have someone along for just this purpose.) If possible, arrange to drive yourself, with the officer beside you on the critical run to the station to post bond. Do not let the law intimidate you in this situation. There are some individual officers who are just dying to play hot-rodder in your Porsche after an arrest in the field. When you detect the trace of a sick smile on the face of one of the uniformed men at the scene, you know you must avoid letting this joker get behind the wheel of your car.

If your car develops mechanical problems, never authorize "Sam's 24-Hour Tow-All" to do the job simply for immediate convenience. Avoid this confrontation by becoming acquainted with the problems involved in capable towing *before* the need is imminent. Services equipped with tilt-bed trucks or trailers offer optimum protection in transit. The experiences of other owners are often helpful and the names of capable wrecking services and individuals to contact can be assembled on a card for your wallet.

The same reasoning applies in case of collision damage. One can only hope that the condition of the automobile after the accident has not been so depreciated by crash damage that improper handling ceases to become a valid consideration. [Illustrated page 108]

FIRE EXTINGUISHERS

As with other accidents, there is no predicting just when, where or how your automobile might burst into flame from a fuel break or an electrical short. In even the brief moment between the fire's outbreak and a successful retardation of the flames, extensive damage can be incurred.

If you wait for outside assistance, you may well be compounding the problem. A side effect of professional fire fighting assistance might be noted. The chemicals fire departments often apply for this type of emergency have been known to permeate carburetors and heads, as well as blister paint finishes. A *controlled,* immediate counterattack can be less traumatic in the aftermath.

Investment in a good fire extinguisher that can be used immediately when needed is insurance against such anguish. Essentially two types of fire extinguishers are effective for use in the Porsche. The CO^2 dry ice format and the Ansul type, using a powder. While unquestionably effective, some powder types have been found to leave a messy residual, a complication that might take repeated cleanings to completely vacate. The equally capable CO^2 leaves little unwarranted mess in the wake.

In the event of a fire, turn off the ignition and remember that the positive battery cable should be disconnected as soon as feasible in the counter-action against any electrically-caused fire, in order to prevent a second ignition.

Carrying a fire extinguisher may also lead to aiding a less fortunate motorist just at the moment of his distress, as well. The satisfaction in rendering help to another is two-fold in the sense that such action would serve as a practice drill.

Catalogs/Accessories & Services

AUTOMOTION
3535 Kifer Road., Santa Clara, CA 95051

BEVERLY HILLS MOTORING
202 S. Robertson Blvd., Beverly Hills, CA 90211

CLASSICS UNLIMITED
6 Gerald Ave., Hicksville, NY 11801

COLGAN CUSTOM MFG.
1945-B Placentia Ave., Costa Mesa, CA 92627

INTERNATIONAL MERCANTILE
P.O. Box 3178, Long Beach, CA 90803

NINE ELEVEN ENTERPRISES
2750 Northhaven, Suite 207, Dallas, TX 75229

PB TWEEKS, LTD., INC.
4410 N. Keystone Ave., Indianapolis, IN 46205

PERFORMANCE PRODUCTS
16129 Leadwell, Van Nuys, CA 91406

STODDARD IMPORTED CARS, INC.
38845 Mentor Ave., Willoughby, OH 44094

TROUTMAN LTD.
3198 L Airport Loop Drive, Costa Mesa, CA 92626

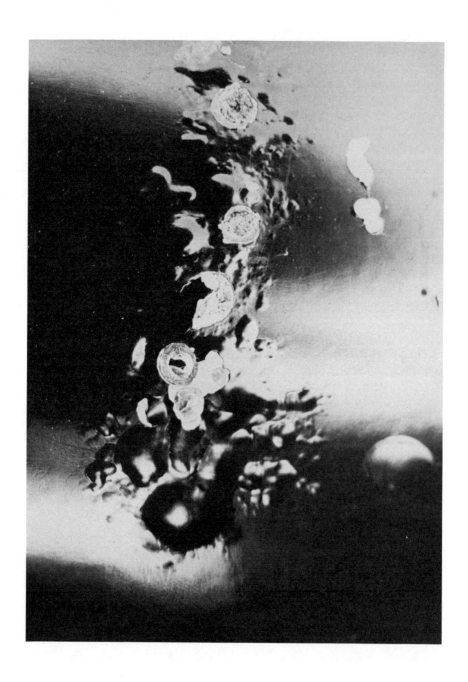

112

5
CORROSION

A white-shoed patron of the wholesale car auction was observed as he began to survey an apparently clean 911T — a rare entity in what the motor trade regards as a disposal marketplace. With its very presence suspect he appeared to take up the challenge. It didn't take him long to discover why the car was being moved in this manner. Dropping to his knees and reaching underside, he exerted mild pressure upward with his bare fist from below the passenger side floorboard.

His companion, who had been busy inside the cockpit, let out an involuntary "Whoop!" as the new-looking carpet flew up from the floor, followed closely by the discoverer's fist as it broke through the shale of a totally corroded-out floor pan.

Even without club affiliation, Porsche owners all share a common bond — *fear of rust*. Dirt traps and reservoirs that harbor moisture are built unavoidably into every car body. Great care in construction can minimize the hazard but just about any Porsche — even after the most deterring measures during manufacture — is vulnerable to the debilitating effects of corrosion.

When an owner anticipates preservation of his Porsche's superior appearance characteristics and highest dollar value through extra years of use, he must confront and conquer the cancer of oxidation. Prevention through careful operation and proper chemical application is less of a problem than removal. The cost of refinishing a rusty Porsche can easily exceed the expense of purchasing a rustfree car at the outset. [Illustrated page 114]

Essential elements in control are the same procedures followed when coping with human ailments: *early detection* and *effective cure*. Keeping a car rustfree while driving it regularly requires conscientious strategy. Although some superficial oxidation is inevitable, there are many products and services designed specifically to help curtail rust-related problems.

Universally, the greatest cause of body and chassis decay is exposure to *salt* — either through coastal exposure or by way of frozen winter roads cleared for travel with NaCl. Abrasion, followed by moisture is a close runner-up. Even when a car is kept out of the notoriously moist night air, it is not unlikely for corrosion to be induced by industrial fallout. In certain locales, many tons of sulphur dioxide can be suspended in the atmosphere at any given time. Mild precipitation is all that is needed to create sulphuric acid, which significantly accelerates the detrimental process.

Capable body shops can replace rocker panels, jack pads, even entire floor panels. But in order to weld in a replacement section there must be something structurally firm to tie to. When the integrity of the whole structure has been compromised by corrosion, panel replacement becomes a game involving the re-establishing of weld points by the addition of improvised fish-plates to provide butting positions. Even when replacement does not involve weakened adjacent areas, *the act of cutting and re-welding compromises the original factory-created structural integrity* of the Porsche body.

Scientifically speaking, corrosion can be physically dangerous to the driver. A research group at Berlin Technical University recently revealed findings that a car having gone through five snow-packed winters has been so weakened structurally that it provides only about *half the tensile strength* of its new twin in withstanding the impact of a collision. Rust imposes another critical problem when holes formed in the car body allow harmful exhaust fumes to filter into the passenger compartment.

Porsche engineers have probably spent more time wrestling with the problem of oxidation than any other firm in an industry where this type of research has traditionally been budgeted sparsely. With the 1981 model year, every Porsche imported into the United States was delivered with a seven-year protection warranty against lower body shell perforation by rust. Initiated in

Limited Anti Corrosion Warranty for New Porsche Vehicles

This Warranty is issued by the Porsche Audi Division of Volkswagen of America, Inc.("Porsche Audi"), the authorized United States importer of Porsche vehicles.

Free repair or replacement of any part of the vehicle body failing within seven (7) years due to rust perforation

1. Porsche Audi warrants to the original retail customer and any subsequent purchaser that every 1981 Porsche vehicle imported by Porsche Audi and sold as a new vehicle to a retail customer will be free from rust perforation, of the vehicle body for a period of seven (7) years after the date of delivery of the vehicle to the original retail purchaser or the date the vehicle was first placed into service, whichever comes first. If any part of the vehicle body is perforated by rust under normal use and service and the vehicle is brought during this period to the workshop of any authorized Porsche dealer in the continental United States, Hawaii or Canada the dealer will, without charge, repair the perforated part or replace it with a new part.

Maintenance required to keep this warranty in effect

2. In order to keep this warranty in effect, the owner must have the vehicle maintained and serviced as prescribed in the Porsche Owner's Manual.

Damage not covered

3. **Porsche Audi is not responsible for rust perforation resulting from:**

(I) **Damage caused by accident, misuse, negligence, alteration, or fire.**

(II) **Improper repair of the vehicle, or**

(III) **Failure to follow recommended maintenance requirements.**

Some states do not allow limitations on how long any implied warranty lasts so the above limitation may not apply to you.

Warranty outside the United States, Hawaii or Canada

4. If the vehicle is brought to an authorized Porsche workshop outside the continental United States, Hawaii or Canada, Porsche Audi's warranty will not be applicable and perforated parts will be repaired or replaced free of charge with new parts only within the terms and limitations of the warranty for new Porsche vehicles in effect in the country where such authorized Porsche workshop is located.

No other warranties made

5. Except for emission control warranties which may be applicable to your vehicle, this warranty and the limited warranty for new Porsche vehicles are in lieu of all other express warranties of Porsche Audi, the manufacturer, the distributor, and the selling dealer. Any implied warranty is limited in duration to the duration of this written warranty. Neither Porsche Audi nor the manufacturer assumes or authorizes any person to assume on its behalf any other obligation or liability.

Consequential damage excluded

6. Porsche Audi is not responsible for loss of time, inconvenience, loss of use of the vehicle, or other consequential damage.
Some states do not allow the exclusion or limitation of incidental or consequential damages, so the above limitation or exclusion may not apply to you.

Other legal rights

7. This warranty gives you specific legal rights, and you may also have other rights which vary from state to state.

Porsche warranty information may be obtained by writing to:

Porsche Customer Assistance
Volkswagen of America, Inc.
818 Sylvan Avenue
Englewood Cliffs, NJ 07632

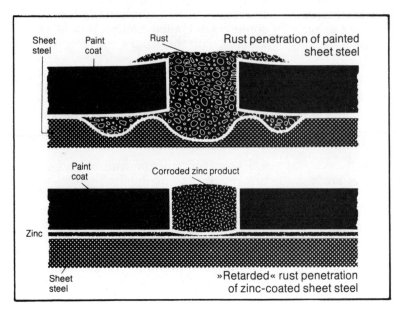

Buildup of protective coats in Porsche painting

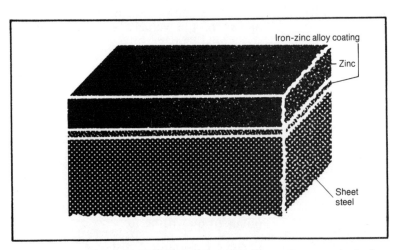

Schematic buildup of fired-zinc sheet metal

118

the early seventies and used extensively in production since the end of 1975, a costly process of hot zinc galvanizing is at the heart of this protective armor.

In the event that this coating is chipped or scratched through to the bare steel, an electro-chemical reaction acts to fill the flawed site with zinc. [Illustrated pages 118, 120] Essentially, zinc acts as a cathode with steel and will, in fact, oxidize also when exposed to air, *but* at a basic rate some 25 times slower than iron.

In collaboration with Thyssen Steel, Porsche settled on this process only after testing more than 200 different sheet materials and coating systems. Included were scores of conventional spray coats and electrolytic dips, as well as others bordering on the exotic. Unconventional inhibitors were also explored with one car painted over an all-inclusive petroleum-based body undercoat which reportedly produced a finish that looked "as though it had been plucked from an orange tree."

Hot galvanizing was found to offer many advantages, among them material thickness. Minimum depth of the treatment chosen is 10 microns, with over 20 microns at areas such as rocker panels and front axle mountings, and 50 microns being used at the rear axle. Prior to forming, each section of sheet metal is dipped in a 940° F. zinc batter. Sections in the splash zone receive a double coat.

The process adds about one ounce per square foot of coverage, resulting in some thirteen pounds of zinc saturation. It also adds more than $100 to the cost of each car in an industry where production costs are more likely to be computed in mills. As Karl Ludvigsen observed, "It [the process] was a bold investment in the reputation and the resale value of the 911."

As the long life ideal follows concrete steps at the comparatively small Porsche firm, other manufacturers have been left with their mouths ajar. One can only appreciate the zinc saturation process in the fullest sense after realizing that it required reworking the tooling dies for 911 bodies at substantial expense. Innovations were also required in welding operations and introduction of special new procedures were required for field repair.

Where other makes tend to seek plastic substitutes for metal, Porsche has moved to stainless steel and aluminum. Applications include the transverse suspension member in the rear, the entire

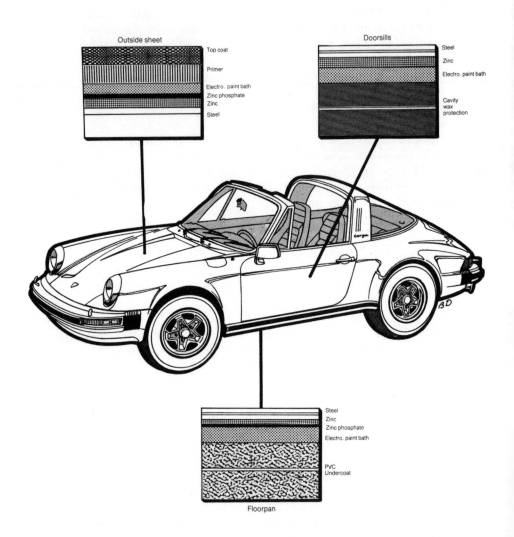

Outside sheet

- Top coat
- Primer
- Electro. paint bath
- Zinc phosphate
- Zinc
- Steel

Doorsills

- Steel
- Zinc
- Electro. paint bath
- Cavity wax protection

Floorpan

- Steel
- Zinc
- Zinc phosphate
- Electro. paint bath
- PVC Undercoat

exhaust system, oil tank and Targa roll bar, with an aluminum coating for the heat exchanger. The continuously more extensive use of aluminum improves both durability and weight economy. Alloy parts include engine and gearbox housings, rear wheel carriers, steering rack, wheels and bumpers. Super durability finishing procedures also extend to efforts in longlife sealing, underbody coating and elaborate electro-prime coating paint preparation.

Through extensive research and costly treatment Porsche has produced a body which should last heartily for a generation and more in any friendly climate. Seven years are assured under guarantee — even at the sea shore. With proper care, owners of post-1975 vehicles may look forward to a casual life expectancy that older model Porsche owners have only obtained by concerted efforts. With the advent of this process one negative note is heard. Surface quality of the ovenbaked enamel used has reportedly not *always* been found up to the superb standard of tradition.

The driver of a late 911 should be aware that the destructive effects of battery acid remain universal. Though this body has been fully coated in the area of the battery compartment, inadvertent boiling over, leaking or shedding will expose the body parts to an acid reaction that tends to ignore the zinc preservative. Inspection of this location should be frequent. A penetrating lubricant, such as LPS #3, can be used to discourage acid build-up on battery connections.

The zinc-coated Porsche also requires special attention in connection with major body repair in order to preserve the integrity of the factory's rust protection capability. The protection can be considerably altered or even destroyed when the sheet metal is reworked. A special zinc dust may be applied as a measure toward reinstating the original protective film.

In the event of extensive damage requiring replacement of whole sections, replacement stampings from the later, processed steel should be used. Let your body man know that you appreciate the difference. Random reports continue to circulate of old stock inventory sometimes being introduced as a more available part for replacement. When the part is the same, the advantages of using the later, rust-processed component in reconstruction can easily be worth a few days extra down time.

The good news for the owner of an earlier car is that such mortality metal parts as rocker panels and fenders are now being stamped from the Thyssen-treated metal from which all later model car parts are produced. So *replacement with the new, anti-corrosive material is possible even on earlier models.*

UNDERCOATING VS. RUSTPROOFING

Preservation experts emphasize the importance of distinguishing between *rustproofing* and *undercoating.* The two terms are not synonymous; each process achieves a result unique to its own properties. They can be employed separately or in conjunction with each other.

Undercoating is a long-accepted process for sound-deadening properties and as insulation against underbody stone damage. Commonly in the aftermarket undercoating is used to obscure the unfinished underside of body repair work.

A "drying-out" characterizes undercoating and renders the semi-flexible asphalt-based concoction almost a liability after a period of time. With the hardening and aging, resilient qualities are lost and the material has a tendency to separate from the surface it was applied to. Although rubber-based undercoatings have come into the market offering advantages including longer service life, apparently some of the sound-deadening effect of asphalt has been lost.

Rustproofing materials are more scientific in design, with formulas developed to adhere to steel in a permanent bond and to penetrate and conform to intricate configurations in steel where undercoating could be regarded only as a general shroud. Superior saturation of remote crevices makes rustproofing the preferred treatment.

Rustproofing compounds seem to break down into two product categories. One is thin in consistency to follow surfaces like a penetrating oil. It provides minimal resistance to abrasion and so is usually used in the coating of inner panels. The other, somewhat heavier in viscosity provides a greater measure of abrasion resistance and is more commonly applied in areas subject to exposure. Both are relatively slow drying and never achieve a tortoise shell-like finish. The thin material remains greasy indefinitely and the latter attains a wax-like texture.

All are inflammable initially and must be handled and applied with certain precautions. After application there is little danger, as the volatile content is a vehicle that usually evaporates in the process.

With either undercoating or rustproofing, the ultimate plus factor is contingent upon the quality of surface preparation and the care exercised in initial application.

UNDERCOATING

The process of undercoating has never lived down its reputation as a cheap, in-house procedure among car dealers through which a healthy up-charge may be tacked onto the sticker price of a new automobile. With the actual undercoating cost marked up five or ten times on the sheet, a "treated" car's price tag can be packed with an increased margin to provide more bargaining room in negotiating the actual selling price.

Unless the Porsche owner can be absolutely certain of his car's dryness and cleanliness — and is aware of the specific conditions peculiar to his undercarriage — *it is not advisable to undercoat with a conventional tar-based material.* [Illustrated page 124] While harsh winters and frequently changing temperatures may make the idea of undercoating seem attractive, consider the pitfalls.

Absolutely proper application is almost impossible. Generally, corners are missed or dirt and moisture already present are coated over, contributing to poor adhesion. (This is little different with a new car.) Once moisture lodges behind the undercoating, the result can rival salt in destructive potential. [Illustrated page 124]

Consider opting for a penetrative oil preservative on the underside in lieu of undercoating. To sense the validity of this approach one need only observe that mariners have always appreciated the effects of light oil in fighting deterioration of metal components on their sea-going vessels. Although these oils express some attraction for dust and provide no insulation, they do offer convenient features.

Clear, light-bodied viscous oils produced under modern technology do not slag, dry sticky, cake up or petrify when properly applied. Preservative oils are compounded not to change form. They differ from ordinary lubricating oils in exhibiting exceptional

penetration, water displacement and comparatively long service life. This protection is widely available in convenient spray cans. Overspray can be removed easily with a dry cloth.

Lubricant coatings are produced widely and are marketed under some names already familiar. WD-40, LPS and CRC come immediately to mind. A variation features the same attributes with the plus of a Teflon base. WGL and Tri-Flon are representative. Both are readily available, with the latter carried by many hardware stores as well as marine supply outlets. Findings indicate that while these Teflon-oriented coatings are more expensive than the plain lubricant coatings, they provide exceptional adhesion, a long-life base and are easily cleaned.

Appropriate application of *a penetrating oil film can add years to the underbody of your Porsche.* It will also act to inhibit aluminum oxidation. Topside, an oil film will forestall pitting in die-cast plated parts such as the side mirror body.

A number of Porsche maintenance experts express a preference for rubber-based materials over straight petroleum compounds. For those areas warranting a tough, abrasion-resistant coating — such as floor panels and wheelhouses — the rubber-based compounds seem to provide an acceptable aftermarket alternative.

Of this genre, 3M's "Body Schutz" (#8864), "Pennzcoat," and "Symtec," are common. Body Schutz (German for *protection*) appears to have secured a widespread acceptance among imported car specialists particularly. While all three products exhibit similar consistency, adherence and flexibility, some users claim 3M's entry leads in convenience of application and in yielding a surface with a perfect affinity for paint.

Body Schutz is dispensed in cans requiring the purchase of a special spray gun of nominal cost. Setup time is comparatively rapid; application and cleanup are uncomplicated. Texture can be varied by over or under stirring or shaking and by adjusting the pressure in application. Severe pressure flattens the effect; lower pressure permits a rougher surface to build up. Thin applications may be repeated to build up a solid protective film. Though drying time is moderate compared with similar products, quite unlike the drying time for paint, there is a substantial waiting period involved. *Conservative individual coats and liberal curing periods are advised.*

Prior to the application of *any* type of undercoating, it is important that you be clinical in preparation. Brush panels, scrape loose deposits, extract grease, vacuum crevices, sand surfaces. *Prepare as if for surgery.* Any residual foreign matter will later act to negate the total effect.

The original undercoating from the factory can create problems in itself. Soap and water applied with a stiff brush can be more effective than one might imagine. After cleaning up the original coating, it is possible to touch up with a clear polyurethane or monopoxy. The revalidation of isolated weak points may sometimes be carried out with such fidelity that a total recoating process may be foregone.

Work on the underbody is most effectively pursued with the aid of a hydraulic lift. If you are not fortunate enough to have access to a lift, it could be worthwhile to seek a new friend in the service garage discipline. (A case of Beck's at the appropriate moment may occasionally be used to open an avenue previously shuttered.)

RUSTPROOFING

Since Porsche's debut among American sports car enthusiasts, valuable experience has been assimilated on the retardation of steel corrosion. As findings continue, important additional strides are still being made. A Porsche body professionally treated to resist corrosion can be expected to last twice as long as an untreated sister car in the same environment.

"It is a fairly extensive process requiring partial disassembly and considerable attention to detail," cautions Chuck Stoddard, the independent expert. There is probably no other protection more comprehensive in insuring the longevity of your vehicle. Imagine eliminating the need later to actually cut metal away and replace sections, simply by buying an effective formula rustproofing which can be applied in the $200 range. As with a paint job, it is the combination of quality materials with skilled application that creates an effective result.

Rustproofing can best be likened to the work involved in painting. Both require tremendous prep before application of the material. It is not unusual for a trained individual to require a time slot of eight to ten hours to assure comprehensive application.

Optimum results are achieved when rustproofing can be applied to a fresh, dry, preferably new car, using special airless atomization spray equipment. Lesser conditions simply require greater prep time. While you can assure optimum results by prefacing the job with preliminary cleanup detailing, it is suggested that you leave the actual application to a carefully selected professional. (For the aspiring do-it-yourself owner, Chuck Stoddard prepared a comprehensive illustrated description of rustproofing procedure which appeared in the January 1975 issue of PCA's *Panorama.*)

The rustproofing shop will secure access to remote areas of your body by drilling holes and then spraying rustproofing compounds into all these voids with a number of dog-legged nozzles. To assure that these access ports are made at the most strategically inconspicious sites, no control is better than being there yourself while this part of the job is underway. Such holes should be capped with plastic plugs after use. (You may want to further obscure these points by spraying these generally bright-colored plugs over in body color.) To obtain a high level of quality make it known to the man on the job that you expect perfection both in preparation and in material coverage.

There are currently a number of independent rustproofing shops throughout the country. Franchise operations are also moving into this field. They are listed in the Yellow Pages but not every rustproofer claiming professional status is capable of being thoroughly effective in protecting your Porsche, either through inadequate experience with the automobile, or possibly through disinclination. (Perhaps he has developed a volume operation with Ford and GM dealers and doesn't want his routine to be interrupted by a challenge.) Seek the operator who is familiar with the Porsche to begin with and guarantees the work on a rustfree used car as well as on a new one. A previously-in-service car requires a two-step process for full effect: a *penetrant* coating followed by a *sealant* coating. All should be pliable in order to yield with the stresses placed on the metal and should ideally be insensitive to temperature changes.

Shop the shops; see what several offer in product, service and *interest* in approaching the Porsche comprehensively. A qualified facility should also provide a printed description of services offered and materials used. Listen to the manager/owner. Observe the types of vehicles that are his principal volume of business. Inquire knowledgably. Carefully review the specifics of guarantees that are offered verbally and in writing to confirm that they correspond. Begin your search for a reputable rustproofer by talking with other owners when you can.

Tuff-Kote Dinol, Inc., is the largest automotive rustproofing company, with an international network claiming more than 3,500 franchised and company operated outlets.

"Waxoyl," marketed through Bilstein, is a European anti-rust compound relatively new to the American market. Geared for the do-it-yourself owner, this product could present a worthy alternative when qualified specialists may appear scarce in your area.

RUST INHIBITIVE PAINTS AND PRIMERS

On an elementary level, rust inhibitive paint products are distinguished from commercial rustproofing products in that they are readily available in paint and automotive stores. Application is generally much less involved. Results vary widely, with the measure of care taken in prep and application again governing the effectiveness of the result. This category encompasses consumer products with familiar names such as Rustoleum, Du Pont, Sherwin Williams, Ditzler, Rinshead-Mason and the like.

Rustoleum Damp Proof Red, compounded from a fish oil base, is commonly used after cleaning and prior to painting areas such as fenders, braces and pans. It is also effective as a primer in touching up nicks, scrapes and scratches. Saturating the door interiors, and other areas revealed only by the removal of trim panels, is a worthwhile step when the total rustproofing process described earlier is to be foregone.

LPS offers a product called "Instant Cold Galvanize" which deposits a 95% pure zinc coating on metal and results in a surface that is heat resistant to 1000° F. The maker claims this material may be used as a superior paint primer.

When refinishing large body portions, or the entire car, it is wise first to evaluate the time-tested performance characteristics of a particular primer. Improper product selection can compromise the finish. Consumer products like Rustoleum and LPS Cold Galvanize are held by many professional refinishers to carry a few long range performance deficiencies if used under an expensive finish. The experienced painter will be acquainted with appropriate primer-topcoat systems of thorough compatability. One commercial primer, Du Pont 825-S Corlar Epoxy Zinc Chromate, is commonly recognized among the pros for providing optimum corrosion resistance with long-life affinity that assures satisfaction in any refurbishing application.

PREVENTION

Though no more of an error has been committed than neglect through innocent ignorance, door bottoms can rust out because drain holes are clogged with debris composed of leaves, twigs, dirt, paper and lint that may have slipped in through the window openings. Even accidents during manufacturing procedures, occasionally may have contributed to this process of door deterioration by inadvertently feeding loose flecks from the door interior sound-proofing effort in Stuttgart to the door wells.

Awareness of factory drain hole locations and a program of keeping them open and functional should be one of the owner's foremost obligations to his Porsche. The stopgap measure of poking a pencil or screwdriver up through accessible holes may act to backwash the sludge on a temporary basis, though only limited matter can be washed out in the process. Survival of original structure really depends upon periodic detachment of the door paneling and removal of all matter blocking the drains, followed by refinishing the inner cavities with an oil film. [Illustrated page 130]

When a car must be subjected to fall foliage and winter rains, the creation of supplementary drain holes may be considered. Substantial water is expelled at the bottom of the hood seal drain channel on many 911 front bumpers, for example. An inconspicious hole can be drilled through the bumper at this collection point to expedite run out.

Front fenders depend upon drain tubes to carry off underside splashes. It is not impossible for this system to become clogged. [Illustrated page 131] Increasing the runoff capacity in this area can be quite worth the effort.

Flotsam accumulates in the area between the oil tank and rear fender almost as a matter of course, because of an inside location that may take weeks to dry out after severe exposure. Here too, the

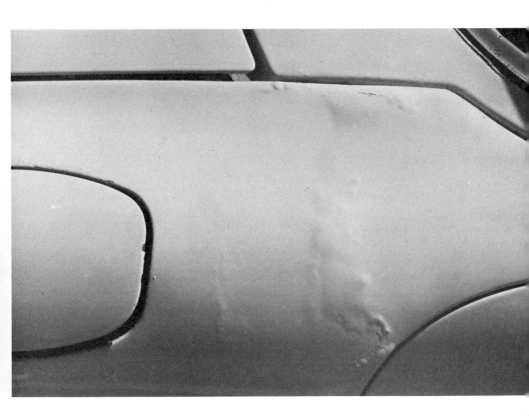

addition of supplementary holes will encourage shorter drying time.

Double panel areas, such as where outer skin meets the inner bulkhead of the fender well, are notorious for collecting mud and other byproducts of the roadway and transforming them into a putty-like substance that retains moisture like a sponge. On a vintage car it is wise to dig out these traps, reprimer and fill with a silicone sealant.

A set of wheelhouse seals constructed of galvanized steel with rubber gaskets at critical contacts have been developed by Hermes Carriage Engineering, a restoration firm in Cambridge, Massachusetts. Claims are that these carefully designed add-ons effectively prevent the accumulation of mud, salt and other corrosives in the nether regions. Configurations have been built for all Porsche models, with complete shield kits and mounting hardware offered in the $100-$200 range.

Worn rubber seals around windows and doors aid and abet trapped moisture. A poor windshield seal will permit water to do serious damage to the cowl and windshield frame, with poor seals in rear glass, side windows and vent panes threatening even greater problems. The Porsche with inadequate seals, when left to the elements unattended could literally fill with water like a bathtub.

Cracked and incomplete seals should be replaced as soon as deterioration is observed. Nothing is to be gained by waiting till they become even less effective. Cracked or loose seals offer only fractional protection from dirt, water and, in turn, corrosion. [Illustrated page 132] Regluing or replacement should be undertaken at the first evidence of failure. Silicone rubber sealer may be used to improve joints where mating parts do not butt as tightly as desired. *Prime condition rubber seals are always seen as one of the marks of a higher value Porsche – and rightly so.*

ENGINE RUST

When a Porsche is subjected only to short distance travels — five mile runs or less — the engine never really attains the temperature level necessary to boil residual water and gas from the crankcase as happens in regular course when shutting down a hot engine. Water vapor is one product of gasoline burning with air. When this passes by piston rings and settles into the crankcase

along with other impurities, the bad news can be major. Inspect the oil filler cap and adjoining areas for rust on a regular basis.

Today's fuels reportedly contain more impurities than in the recent past. The introduction of an otherwise negligible quantity of water in an injected Porsche's fuel system can result in disaster. Methanol-based formulas have been developed to combat this problem by enabling water to mix with gasoline sufficiently so it may pass through the injection system without causing damage. Use of such an additive on regular schedule may even assure ultimate fuel performance on a Porsche with regular carburetion. In aircraft maintenance mild phosphoric acid solutions have been used to clean and seal fuel tanks. Availability of certain compounds is regional. A survey may be required in your area.

RUST DETECTION

Characteristic of the corrosion process is that it will never become less of a problem than it is on the day of discovery. Rust can compound other unanticipated problems, sometimes resulting in terminal ills. Postponing repair or replacement of a pan section till your passenger slips a shoe through the floor should not be considered as an option. In addition, the more extensive the reconstruction required, the more likelihood there will be of deviation from factory specifications in structural integrity and appearance when the restoration is completed. It is not unrealistic to project that the cost involved in quality work of this nature may legitimately exceed current market value of the automobile.

Earlier cars, built under less sophisticated preventive measures, are naturally apt to reveal their rust faults first. General inspection should be made on any Porsche built before the end of 1975, with very detailed scrutiny recommended for a car manufactured prior to 1969.

The pattern is all too familiar. [Illustrated pages 134, 136-137] Rocker panels are often the first to go, along with the battery locale and the crossmember located at the tow hook. The rear of the sills back to the aft torsion bar mounts are nearly as vulnerable. Heater boxes, door edges, and lock and antenna surrounds display rot with regularity. Rust building from the top side is often found in the leading edge of the front hood and in the pockets at the bottom of the headlight frames. Careless remounting of garnish items, such

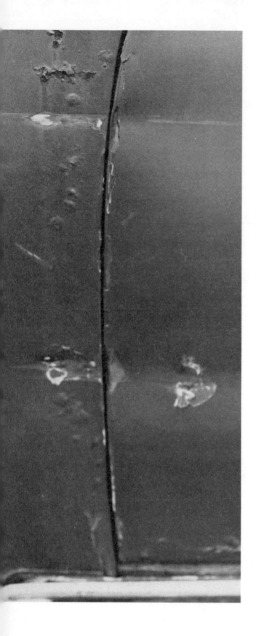

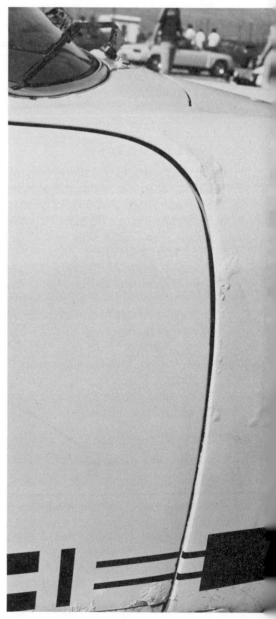

136

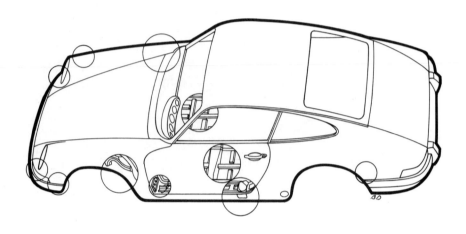

138

as outer handles, trim, badges and lettering have sometimes fractured the paint in the process, resulting in chipping, and in turn early corrosion.

Bear in mind that *areas in which body repairs have been previously rendered are more likely to rust* than sections where virginal surfaces have been retained.

Welcome the first opportunity to become familiar with the underside of your Porsche, utilizing a strong lamp while the car is on a lift. The degree of overall solidarity and originality will be readily evident. The prime rust area underneath will probably be detectable first in the notorious battery compartment region (equally susceptible even on recent production) and extending toward the front struts. Jack points and heat ducts should be examined closely. The stresses incurred by *those areas functioning as locating elements for suspension components tend to promote rust* practically from Day One.

Any undercoating material, whether original or applied by a previous owner, may conceal problem areas in the incubation stage of corrosion. If certain clues lead you to suspect hidden deterioration, begin by scrutinizing closely those areas where rust has been known to originate. [Illustrated page 138]

Any simple prod may be employed to locate festering points. The blade of a screwdriver or chisel will be safer to handle and less damaging than a pointed pick or scribe. Aim the tip at questionable points and simply tap the handle with your palm. Inside, remove the carpets and proceed in the same manner.

When it is necessary to remove the undercoating be forewarned: *there is no easy way to strip this material.* Scrapers of the pneumatic variety can accomplish the task, but they are also capable of inflicting heavy damage when only slightly misdirected. Wirebrushes and scrapers with interchangable heads are used most effectively, especially with a variety of shapes, lengths and widths to complement every nook and cranny underside.

Once the coating has been removed, thoroughly clean the area with steel wool and solvent. Although they resemble corrosion, the rust-*colored* residual stains from the petroleum-based coating should not cause alarm.

REMOVAL OF RUST

The primitive Woods Indian knew that he had to plug the hole in his canoe before he could begin to bail the water out of it with any success. Corrosion, too, must be terminated before effective action can be taken to prevent its further spread.

Many different metals have been used in the construction of the Porsche for as many special reasons where weight-saving, extra strength, or resistance to elements may have been prime considerations. Body panels have been shaped from aluminum and from steel. On a limited production machine such as the 1958 356 Carrera GT, for example, doors and deck lid stampings utilize aluminum with the balance of body panels developed from steel. Stainless steel, magnesium, brass, sophisticated castings from powdered metals and die-cast materials have also been used.

In the spectrum of metallurgy, alloys used for particular attributes do not all respond to the same treatment that may be attended to steel. Nor are they susceptible to the same forms of deterioration.

Tools and chemicals commonly used with iron and steel may act to rapidly destroy certain other metals. One must be able to distinguish and act accordingly.

Elementary as it may seem, a simple magnet test is universally effective in determining iron from "other than" among specific component parts. When a magnet hesitates to cling to a section known to be formed of steel, however, paint covering the suspect area must be removed to properly appraise the quality or severity of the lead or bondo fill.

Rust-removing concoctions run the gamut in today's market. Many experts agree that generic products using time-proven phosphoric and muriatic acids remain among the most effective available.

An unorthodox service product which claims to remove rust *without* acid or sandblasting while establishing its own primer surface is available from Rusticide Products Co., under the trade name "Ospho." When applied to a rusted panel prepared by wire brushing it will, reportedly, convert iron oxide into inert phosphate with the action complete when a blackened appearance remains after a mild white residue is brushed away.

140

The product chosen should have a primary reputation for performance in your specific problem area. Formulations offered as jellies or pastes facilitate application in vertical or overhead regions.

If rust is detected early in its formative stage, effective removal can be achieved with "Rust Bioux," a non-toxic, biodegradable product that is applied as a spray and rinsed off with water. Relatively new to the American market, this product claims an origin in Scandanavia and is said to have enjoyed widespread acceptance in Europe. It is supplied with an impressive unconditional guarantee. Details are available from the Starshine Group.

The following companies are representative in providing products developed specially to help negate effects of corrosion. All offer descriptive material on request.

ACP, P.O. Box 130, Randolph, WI 53956

Allan Marine, 91 Industry Court, Deer Park, NY 11729

Beck Chemical, Inc. 3350 W. 137th St., Cleveland OH 44111

CRC Chemicals Division, C. J. Webb, Inc., Limekiln Pike, Dresher, PA 19025

Dew-Coated Lubricants, P.O. Box 5755, Chicago, IL 60680

Fine Organics, Inc., 205 Main St., Lodi, NJ 07644

Flitz International, 3149 Buckingham Rd., Sturtevant, WI 53177

Graf Enterprises, 640 Niagara Street, St. Catharines, Ontario, Canada L2M 3R3

Intercoastal Paint Co., Dundalk Station, Baltimore, MD 21222

LPS Research Labs, Inc., 2050 Cotner Ave., Los Angeles, CA 90025

Magnus Division, Economics Laboratories, Inc. Osborn Bldg., St. Paul, MN 55102

Marne Development & Research Corp., 381 Park Ave., South, New York, NY 10016

Nalco Chemical Co., 180 N. Michigan Avenue, Chicago, IL 60601

Oil Center Research, 211 Rayburn, Lafayette, LA 70501

Okun Co., Inc. 109-02 Van Wyck Expressway, Jamaica, NY 11420

Permatex Co., Inc., Box 1350, West Palm Beach, FL 33402

Phillips Mfg. Co., 7334 N. Clark St., Chicago, IL 60626

Radiator Specialty Co., 1400 W. Independence Blvd., Charlotte, NC 28201

Resins Research Corp., 1989 Byberry Road, Huntingdon Valley, PA 19006

Rock Chemical Corp., 5-40 45th Ave., Long Island City, NY 11101

Rust Lick, Inc. 755 Boylston St., Boston, MA 02116

Rusticide Products Co., 3125 Perkins Ave., Cleveland, OH 44114

Starshine Group, 924 Anacapa St., Santa Barbara, CA 93101

Testing Systems, Inc. 2826 Mt. Carmel Ave., Glenside, PA 19038
Unimetrics, Inc., 23 West Mall, Plainview, NY 11725
WD-40 Co., 4390 Napa St., San Diego, CA 92110
Woodhill Chemical Sales Corp., 18731 Cranwood Parkway, Cleveland, OH 44128
Woolsey Marine Industries, Inc., 201 E. 42nd St., New York, NY 10017

Most of these compounds have been developed to attack iron oxidation while reacting passively to the parent metal. This selective activity is common among rust removers, with phosphoric acid often relied upon as the active ingredient. Products used industrially often include action which leaves a "protective" film or coating on the cured surface. Desirability of this feature depends upon the type of refinishing the surface is scheduled to receive.

In the curing of large areas on doors, fenders, decklids and other removable components, the services provided by commercial metal processing franchises such as Redi-Strip and 3M may present a viable alternative consideration. Be aware beforehand, that while claiming to purge the material of all deteriorating matter that is no longer structually sound, the process does in fact siege everything nonferrous (including the body lead) at the blighted site. As a consequence, after commercial stripping, there may be need for special extra attention to restore some surfaces to the quality desired.

6
BODY WORK

Preserving Intrinsic Worth

Ron certainly didn't feel that his asking price for the '56 Carrera was unreasonable. After all, it wasn't a common model and there were probably more people out there wanting one than there were existing cars. He watched confidently as the prospective buyer — who had traveled more than three hundred miles just to inspect the Porsche — listened attentively to the original four cam 1500 GS engine while he caressed the carefully preserved leather trim. From all appearances he seemed impressed.

A few moments later, striding to the rear, the knowledgable prospect produced a small magnet from his pocket. Expert investigation of the pre-T-2 series steel body surfaces followed. It was something new to Ron. Beginning at the engine cover he moved forward far enough to become acquainted with the headlight buckets. After a survey of only the left side the caller had reached a decision.

Muttering a less than cordial "Thanks for your time," he left abruptly.

Why had this potential buyer so arrogantly rejected Ron's seemingly desirable 356A? The magnet had revealed that body panels on the driver's side harbored large investments of body filler, and subsequent tapping confirmed they were not composed of lead. Plastic filler in any quantity signals collision damaged panels or rot, or both, and indicates a deviation from fidelity during reconstruction. As a Porsche enthusiast of some experience this prospect had simply wanted no part of a "bondo bomb."

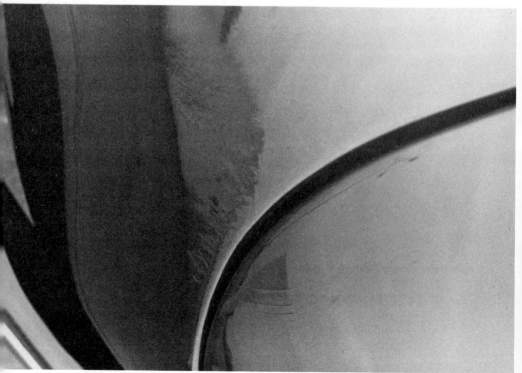

Ron had never known of the filler. At least for the future he had learned an important lesson from this encounter: Know a car *before* you buy it.

Superficially, lead and plastic as fillers serve the same objective, but similarities end there. Properties in handling and long term results are quite different.

Plastic will adhere to any metal without much regard for surface preparation, even clinging to corroded members, *for a while.* Plastic can and does, as a consequence, fall out, flake off, recede in joints and contours, and even crack — all with total disregard for the megabucks that may have been spent otherwise on the paint job.

Along with the gradually contracting properties of plastic filler, the polyurethane foam, zinc gauze and aluminum tape sometimes used under the substance in the re-creation of panels have been known to buckle and shrink, distorting surfaces and creating pockets for new corrosive action. [Illustrated page 144] Though not up to par in dimensional stability for permanence, plastic filler repair — not requiring any special talent to handle — has found its place in the Fairmont/Vega/Gremlin body repair field where runout life expectancy, however renewed, remains predictably brief.

Conditions in today's economy have tempted an occasional Porsche owner to consider the bondo shortcut. A plastic repair will generally run no more than two-thirds the cost of a metal and lead job. The saving is not so much in material as in cutting down on the number of labor hours required to yield an *acceptable-looking* job.

Lead solder must be applied in accordance with exacting procedure or it will express no adhesion at all. Lead will not stick to rust.

Few real Porsche people will accept extensive bondo-type repair as the equal of releaded work, in which finesse in refinishing can be carried out to the level of perfection desired. The Porsche preservationist who holds continuing value foremost has no choice. He knows that the digression from original specifications associated with the bondo-type filler repair may contribute directly to substantial dollar depreciation.

While the restoration of engine or transmission requires technical aptitude, the availability of conventional replacement parts

and the specifics of the exchange permit such work to be carried out as a relatively tangible procedure.

Properly rectifying neglected body work in contrast, is a more elusive task than renewing mechanical components. Buying the services of a mechanic can be a predictable quantity. Harnessing the creative forces of an artist may be less cut and dried.

The unrivaled supremacy of the original Porsche factory jigs, assembly procedures and trim applications are no longer to be enjoyed once a car leaves the factory. Resurrection of physical shapes and surfaces in this after-factory service climate frequently gravitates to an endeavor of subjective nature. The "eye" of the metal man becomes all-important in a field in which truly qualified body surgeons are few and far between. It is not uncommon for a finished reconstruction to fail to meet the owner's expectations.

The shop chosen for Porsche body reconstruction, large or small, should be selected only after a comprehensive search. Compare facilities, not so much for size but for space organization and cleanliness in working detail. Observe work in progress. Obtain references from the shop manager and review finished work after some months of service in the field.

When you settle for a reputable shop with an appreciation for your desire to retain the clean lines and value that are built into your car, you will very likely have also discovered a shop that does not use plastic matter in its work. The master metal man, given sufficient time (and that's where the extra cost comes in), is capable of reworking bent metal and even hammer-welding in new pieces without using any filler at all.

When corrosion extends beyond the surface, the best alternative, short of panel replacement, is accomplished by cutting out the malignant area and welding in a clean replacement section. [Illustrated page 148] Should the nature of deterioration or damage dictate extensive *reforming,* it is always better to opt for replacement with a new panel. Unfortunately, not all cosmetic components are available off-the-shelf for all models.

Whenever damage to a fender or a door assembly is so extensive that an entire panel requires re-establishing and a *new* replacement is not readily available a better job will result from substitution of a straight piece secured from a Porsche being dismantled for parts. When the replacement part is free from previous

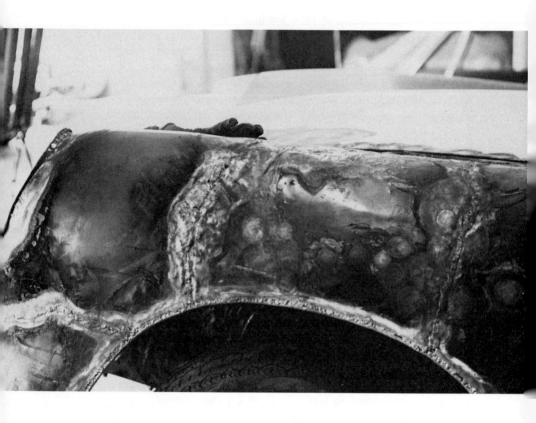

repairs, this solution is most effective. Installation of a panel that has been subject to restoration at some previous time(s) may not provide perfect alignment and edge tolerances, and may otherwise result in a disappointing job.

This devaluating experience can usually be prevented when the owner is permitted to inspect used parts before authorizing their incorporation in his Porsche's reconstruction. Often a selection of parts, each with its own relative originality, may be available to a Porsche body reconstruction shop. Only by conveying expectations of pristine quality and workmanship at the *first* visit can the owner be sure of securing *prime* used replacement sections for his car. When the customer's insistence for superior work is not established for the body shop to grasp *before* the work is started, it generally becomes a matter of requiring that the job be *redone* . . . a traumatic encounter for all parties, at best.

Ironically, while certain early model Porsches are now valued higher than later cars, a running belief in general body shop practice persists that owners of older cars are somehow deserving of lesser treatment. It is true that sheet metal parts availability usually diminishes as an average car grows older and drops to marginal sales value. So it is that often the average body shop's unconscious discrimination results in the pawning off of tweaked panels and the liberal use of plastic filler. From this encounter the owner's vintage model emerges with evidence of marginal quality, both in material and in repair effort.

Greater hope exists in the Porsche specialist's body shop where the owner's language is "spoken" and older cars are rightfully venerated. As the owner of *any* Porsche, you are entitled to a character of repair work that results in a car that is *not depreciated* by the restoration effort. *Nothing less should be acceptable.* Insist on perfection from Moment One in dealing with the shop you have chosen. Follow this up by insisting on correction of any faults in the reconstruction work during progress checks and, finally, in the finished job *before tendering payment*. You have no other stick to swing. Consider yourself lucky if you come out ahead in *any* dealing with the average body shop; do everything in your power to come out *even*. When the shop thinks of you as "one hell of a bastard" when you finally drive away with the job you wanted, chances are you have extracted their best efforts.

Not long ago Lee's daily service 912 incurred collision damage to one front fender. He drove out to a particular shop that publicized itself as a high quality Porsche repair specialist, even though this necessitated a 100-mile-plus round trip. Two estimates were written: one for repair of the original fender and one for replacement of the part, using an allegedly straight (but unseen) "used" fender.

The estimate for repairing the damaged piece carried a savings of six labor hours over the estimate entailing replacement. A parts item of $300, plus sales tax on that amount, appeared on the quotation predicated on replacement.

A decision was made in favor of the costlier replacement job. When the car was dropped off on a second trip, as appointed, Lee, having a curiosity interest, requested that the old fender be preserved and returned.

Several days later he returned to the shop to inspect progress. Fresh primer seemed to indicate that everything was moving on schedule. Instilled with the trust from what had appeared bona fide recommendations, Lee assumed that all was well. Before departing he reminded the proprietor again that he really did want to see the old fender. He was informed that it had been temporarily stored up in the rafters — "out of the way" — with the shop operator adding that it would be taken down and made available at the end of the week when the car was ready to pick up.

The 912 owner arrived at the time agreed, only to discover the "finished" work unacceptably disappointing. The rating the customer had held for this body shop dropped like an elevator with a broken cable. Gaps were conspiciously misaligned; mismatched welts glared prominently; the rubber seal at hood edge was peeking out in a pinch; brand new nicks in the freshly refinished and rubbed out area (caused, it was later admitted, by dropping a screwdriver on the finished job) had been unsportingly obscured only from the blind by daubs of paint. Distrust began to fester.

When confronted with a reiteration of the visible flaws, the shop hesitantly agreed to rework the job to alleviate the obvious, though relations had become strained by Lee's "demanding" specifications. In an atmosphere now charged with distrust, the desire to see the old fender was brought up once again. When the proprietor returned after several minutes of "searching," he declared that the fender had been thrown out. One of his metal men called over at this point in summation, "It was of no use to us and it wouldn't be of any use to you."

For the fourth run to the distant body shop to pick up the corrected car several days later, the enthusiast had again drafted a friend for this third excursion in which two drivers had been necessary. This time the 912 appeared to be as ordered and the owner began to look for a convenient spot in which to write out his check, which he was prepared to back up with a check cashing bank card and a Visa card. It was then he was informed, for the first time, that the shop would not accept a personal check. Courtesies were now no longer being exchanged. It was already late afternoon and banks were closed. For a long moment it appeared that a fifth trip might be necessary to regain possession of the Porsche. The day was saved only by the good fortune that his companion was traveling with a very liquid wallet that day.

Once back on home ground Lee took the time to inspect the fender repair closely for the first time. It was then that he recognized familiar signs — identifiable flaws outside the realm of the repair. It was indeed the original fender, nicely repaired now to all appearances. Underside, the fender confirmed the suspicion in a maze of pieces and patches.

His quotation had shown, and he had paid for a replacement fender. The job had been performed on the basis of the original written estimate. No itemized bill had been presented. Unfortunately for the record, the Porsche owner had neglected to request one. This shop, in spite of a widespread reputation for conscientious involvement, had performed a major con and cover-up. For all purposes the perpetrators were home free.

Similar experiences and a host of unsatisfied customers everywhere attest to the need for careful scrutiny of body repair work. It is essential for the repair customer to be sufficiently educated in the specialized ways and means of this particular trade to obtain the full measure of his intent.

152

7
PRESERVATION

Retaining those Original Attributes

Stuart drove his 912E out of a Los Angeles showroom in May, 1976. Brian took delivery of his 912E from a Minneapolis dealer later the same month. The two cars were similarly equipped and both men observed maintenance by the book and saw that their cars were washed regularly. Neither was to incur collision damage during the course of low mileage original ownership.

Ironically, the car that was kept in winter wonderland appreciated in value, while the sunny California car depreciated from its original cost.

The difference was in the washing. Brian did his own detailing in the shade of a spreading chestnut tree in his back yard. Stuart, who happened to be the operator of a string of commercial car washes, availed himself of his ready facilities almost daily. Beyond switching brushes to slow speed, little thought was given to the brutally predictable effects that pressurized steam, harsh detergents and comparatively insensitive mechanical rollers and brushes would have on his very special car. It never occured to him that damage would also result from those multi-purpose drying rags that sometimes remained in the hands of his employees for a whole shift.

As time passed, Stuart did realize under disturbing circumstances that what he had regarded as a perk of management was actually costing him dearly. Instead of considering correction he decided simply to sell. His well-phrased classified ad attracted prospects like orange blossoms attract bees. It was then that he watched prospects grimace at the sight of a scratched windshield, blemished fender flares, strangely mottled alloys and paint sand-polished to a matt finish.

A sale was finally consumated only by deducting substantially more than the estimated cost of replacing glass and carrying out proper refinishing. Stuart also had come to realize that the extra care required to maintain pride in a Porsche was not for him. His next car was a Capri.

Brian has already purchased two more Porsches — a 356 and a 911SC — and plans to buy a 924 for his wife are on the horizon. Although his first, the 912E, had followed the snow plow on many a morning, it was in outstanding condition the day he parted with it.

Stuart learned the hard way. *You* do not have to. If you must submit your Porsche to conveyor-line cleaning, disfiguration can be reduced by following simple precautions.

1. *Personally drive the car to the starting point.*
2. *Request that the car be run through on the slowest cycle or have the brushes retracted.* (Most control panels are equipped with what the trade refers to as a "slow button." This electronic regulator is designed to decrease the RPM of the brushes for cleaning of new paint jobs and other sensitive finishes. Operations without this feature can usually put the brushes on a retract mode which keeps them from coming into contact with the body.)
3. *Personally drive the car away from the finish point.*
4. *Supervise the hand detailing.* (Insure that the rags used on the wheels don't make contact with glass, etc.)

Much can be learned about a car washing enterprise by first observing service on cars other than your own. Do the employees treat Mrs. Jones' 450SL the same as Mrs. Smith's Impala? Watch a few go through before committing your Porsche to the same treatment.

Make it a point to ask the proprietor if rocker panel and wheel brushes are fed with a solvent type cleaner. Many outfits advertise this feature as a bonus. It is not. The automated spray guns almost always misdirect the volatile material.

Complying with a growing necessity in the commercial car washing industry to soften a generally ill reputation among owners of quality cars, one leading manufacturer of automated equipment recently chose to spotlight the temperate effect of its machinery.

An elaborate brochure was circulated in the trade featuring the Porsche with statements like ". . . the equipment that washes the finest exotics in the world with tender loving care. [Illustrated page 156] It is good to know that the mechanized wash industry is conscious of the problem and trying to do something about it.

Many factors other than improper washing act to downgrade the appearance of any automobile. Rain, snow, stones, salt, sap, birds, insects, oils, solvents, soot and tar, as well as sun and temperature changes and the neighbor's cats, are ready antagonists. Nonetheless, preservation begins with proper washing.

A regular schedule is best, with frequency depending upon whether your car is in daily service or subjected only to occasional runs. A rule of thumb is that when the Porsche *looks like* it needs a bath, it is already past due. The reasoning: the need to scrub entrenched film requires more effort and subsequently shortens the life of the finish.

In some circumstances washing should be by reflex, such as after travel on a salted roadway. Your Porsche will also require more frequent washing when you live near salt water where micro-corrosion begins immediately unless it is neutralized.

Locate your car out of direct sunlight and permit it to cool before beginning. Recalling that old refrain about "Only mad dogs and Englishmen . . ." recognize also that hot surface washing causes spotty drying. Washing is hazardous in frosty weather except when it is possible to *completely* dry the vehicle. Hairline cracks are created by the effects of freezing dampness.

When a Porsche is used in the bitter cold of a long, white winter, there is more to washing than considering the fact that cold contracts. While continuous attention to the underside is imperative, car washing topside should not be too frequent. Excess flow inside doors can remain for weeks when it freezes. In winter it is better to permit dirt to accumulate — being careful not to rub anything against it — till a warm, dry day, to facilitate better drying of the inner sides of hood, doors and deck lid. *Door rot,* the result of frozen captive water, is perhaps the Number One problem among cars used in winter.

The eastern U.S. Porsche underside, alluded to above, should be kept neutralized continuously. The high pressure self-service car wash, where you deposit a coin and take up the nozzle in hand,

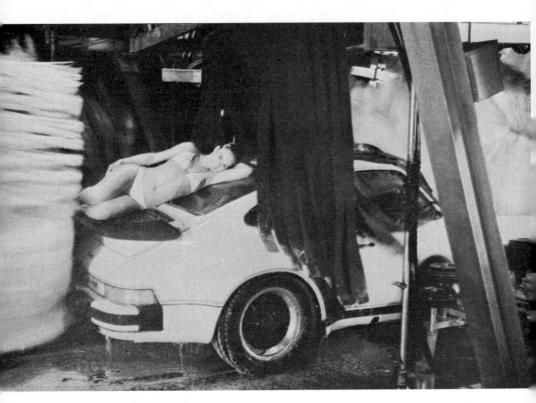

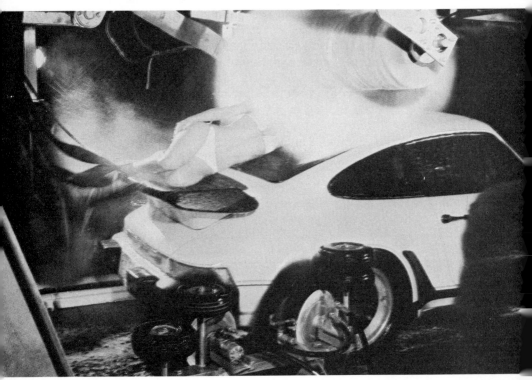

is a good place to maintain the undercarriage. Strong detergents acting with a forceful jet stream are great for tough road deposits but can undermine painted edges.

Plain cold or cool, preferably soft, water can be used to remove loose surface dirt and dust sufficiently well for routine light-touch cleaning of the topside. A well-waxed finish is best cleaned with a soft sponge and plain water.

Always rinse the surface with water before any rubbing takes place to prevent marring the finish. *A dry cloth should never be used to clean your car's surface, not even a treated cloth sold for this purpose.* Even the finest build-up of grit will produce subtle scratches on paint or glass when redistributed by rubbing with a dry cloth.

When the finish is really dirty, a *mild* car washing liquid is suggested. Non-detergent dishwashing liquids work; moderation is essential. One should be leary of detergent products that also claim a wax feature. The detergent aspect usually suffices, but the alleged "wax" more likely is actually silicone or mineral oil that deposits a thin film. Essentially, this is often the material applied by commercial car washes during their "waxing" stage. The protection this coating provides is of fleeting duration and very little sheen actually results.

Common detergents have even been proven detrimental to the painted surface. Some owners have courted disaster by chasing tar deposits with solvents such as kerosene. This predictably, erodes the Porsche's finish. Use careful judgement in dealing with the obstinate splash stains that collect in skirt areas of the body. Preparation should include reduction of clinging masses by picking and chipping. Carefully confine use of prepared tar remover to the immediate spots where absolutely necessary.

Begin washing by watering down the top part of the car, avoiding a pressure stream by utilizing a garden hose without a nozzle. Soak the surface repeatedly. Dip a large, soft sponge in a bucket of clean tepid water or very diluted car washing suds and cover the Porsche's surfaces with a light, circular motion of the sponge, using limited force. Avoid the greater pressure that would cause any impurities to act as a scouring agent. The protective finish on the Targa roll bar is among the body surfaces most easily scratched.

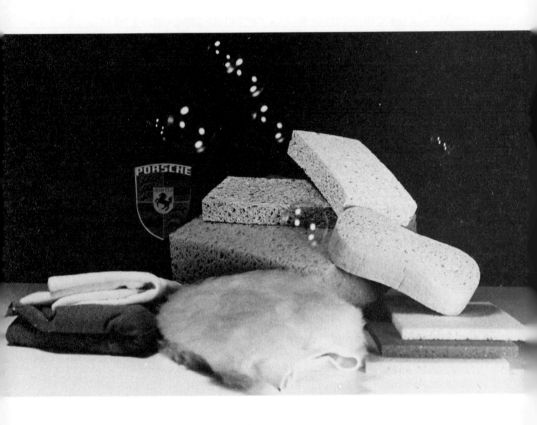

Abrasive powder cleansers should never touch your car's exterior finish. Difficult stains and spots can be removed by placing a little baking soda directly on the subject area. Moistened baking soda scours without scratching.

Maintaining the sponge while washing is critical. Squeeze it out often, dipping it into a rinse bucket before returning for a new load from the washing mix. After a sponge has accidentally fallen onto the ground or pavement it must be thoroughly washed before being returned to the job.

A garden hose without a nozzle provides sufficient rinsing without the danger of jet stream damage. To protect the Porsche's finish from the brass hose tip install a bumper end. Cut two holes slightly under the outside diameter of the hose in opposite sides of a tennis or racquet ball. Force thread the hose through the ball, positioning it just inside the end.

A natural chamois is the time honored "cloth" for washing, wiping and drying, but terry cloth also serves. *Paper toweling should remain in the kitchen.*

Porsche alloy wheels, like the Targa overhead bar, have been anodized or otherwise treated to preserve their luster. Caustic solutions may discolor them. Beware of wheel cleaners. Many are potent enough to remove the black paint that highlights the burnished spokes. Metal polishing compounds are abrasive and must be avoided. The safest way to care for alloys and the Targa bridge is to exercise restraint. Anodizing is best washed with soft sponges and mild soaps.

Following washing and drying of the body, underbody and tires, direct your attention to the windows, lamps and mirrors. Window cleaners are acceptable, as are concoctions using the household standby ammonia. One thing to remember in regard to glass cleaning is the necessity for using clean cloth surfaces continuously. Another point is that window cleaners commonly contain mild acids, indicating that glass cleaning should be a dry-as-you-go procedure. When accidentally permitted to stand after spraying, this type of cleaner may do enough surface etching so that stains are formed which can be reduced only by hard polishing.

A number of Porsche people are moved to wax their vehicles as a cosmetic finish. The procedure is also believed to protect the paint from weather, oxidation and minor contacts.

A clean, smooth surface reflects light. Grime and related traffic films break down light reflections causing the finish to appear dull. As Porsche paint ages and is exposed to diverse elements, it starts to deteriorate — often unnecessarily. The finish begins to collect dirt faster and finally to chalk, the result of a breakdown in pigmentation.

The relative value of a Porsche is continuously assured when original paint is preserved. Repainting should never be prompted by the first signs of dulling or cracking. A few hairlines in an original finish are even regarded by some enthusiasts as lines of character or "maturity." *Strive to hold that original finish as long as possible.*

When a finish has faded or chalked, a pre-wax product should be used first. These paint restoring compounds are provided both in liquid and paste forms. Pre-wax cleaners use light abrasive action to "wipe" away subdued surface scratches and stubborn dirt that washing did not remove. Since a small fraction of the finish is actually removed with each application, restraint in frequency of use should be observed. Every wax job should not be prefaced with a cleaner treatment.

More highly abrasive material such as rubbing compound should only be used to remove deep surface scratches. These compounds are capable of removing several layers of paint. Controlled use is recommended to avoid adverse effects from over-zealous rubbing.

COMBINATION PRODUCTS

Dozens of car care products are compounded to include both a polishing material and a protective coating. Combination offerings vary in form from paste and liquid to aerosol spray.

While this material cannot be built-up by multiple applications to achieve the protective effect that several coats of abrasive-free wax provides, some owners whose vehicles have not begun to chalk claim results justify its use over the double work of traditional two-step procedure. Others report that initial gloss can be deceiving and that both shine and protective qualities are of short duration.

The primary edge attained with the dual purpose product seems to result at the time of application through requiring less effort. It works best on young finishes. Those that have seen aging and neglect prove less responsive. Traditional two-step polishing and protecting operations remain the only effective method for restoring dull, chalky surfaces.

WAXING

Proper wax application is a laborious, time-consuming, largely hand process, but many owners feel the protective rewards make it worthwhile. Advocates point out how it forms a seal to protect both finish and metal trim from natural and photochemical atmospheric contamination and how it floats minor impurities from the car's surface during simple hosing.

Various compounds have been used with some success. Non-abrasive wax products can be found as hard cake, paste, liquid and even in the convenience package of an impregnated applicator pad. An ingredient common among the best is *carnauba wax,* a hard, brittle yield from the Brazilian fan-leaved palm, with a quality that works equally well on all types of finish.

Wax should always be applied to a rag rather than to the finish. A uniform circular motion of light to medium pressure with consistent coverage brings the superior result. In their reach for additional claims to elevate a particular wax above others, ad writers have occasionally suggested that a product may even be applied in direct sunlight. It is best to discount this claim. *Waxing should always be done out of the sun.*

The advantage with carnauba wax is its relatively high melting point among wax materials, a property providing superior durability, as well as gloss. It does tend to "set" soon after application, requiring that coverage be made in stages. Each small area or panel should be waxed and finish polished before advancing.

When wiping off the dry wax, use a different clean-soft-dry rag for removal and preliminary buffing. When moving to a new area, change to a new part of the rag. *The secret of outstanding wax application is access to a virtually unlimited supply of clean cloths.*

Sheepskin probably provides the most effective texture for bringing up maximum gloss in the final buffing stage. If the job must be attempted on a humid day, a small amount of cornstarch on the polishing cloth counteracts undesired moisture and aids in attaining optimum brilliance.

If a buffer disc is used in conjunction with a regular drill motor, special caution must be taken in every moment of use. Does this make-shift substitution represent a real saving? What you have in your hands, in effect, is a high speed circular saw. Professional buffing motors, in contrast, work at low rpms. When a buffer is to be used regularly, investment in the proper equipment is as important as taking the time to do the job right. For the occasional job, a buffer can be rented.

Many enthusiasts make a concerted effort to wax and polish their cars at least three times a year. Actual frequency depends upon the region a car is driven in, how often it is washed, and whether it is protected from extremes of climate. When your Porsche's surface is insulated from air and moisture by proper waxing — which generally means several coats — the effort should provide long life, if it is not left in blasts of sunlight for extended periods. In a shaded, temperate environment, a newer car may only require wax once every two or three years. Once introduced, however, maintenance is necessary. If the later follow-up waxing is delayed, a more abrasive polish will be required to restore the paint.

Appreciating that the painted surface actually becomes minutely thinner with each wax prep should provide the incentive to act before the necessity for a redo becomes imminent. Effort, as well as paint, will be saved.

Though the procedure outlined has gained time-honored acceptance, according to some, wax may not be the last word in paint preservation. Another trend of thought contends that a high quality enamel or lacquer finish is best maintained through an approach not unlike feeding fine leather with conditioning oil. This theory was developed from the premise that deterioration of automobile paint results from a natural drying out of the oils used in the color pigmentation. Some say that satisfaction can be extended by periodically replenishing proper oils and compounds rather than by sealing the surface with a carnauba wax. Advocates claim that wax does not allow the original chemical composition to breathe freely and thus causes irreversible deterioration under the carnauba coating.

Practice of this technique is contingent upon availability of the proper materials and consideration of the use to which the vehicle is subject. Providing very little protection from the elements and requiring regular reapplication to maintain an acceptable gloss, "replenishment" is probably most suitable to the show car that sees limited regular driving.

Polishes prepared for brightwork like bumpers and trim cannot be expected to provide the rust protection obtained from a wax. As time passes, diecast parts will develop pits and plated steel will develop rust spots, unless exposed surfaces are protected. [Illustrated page 164] When a chrome polish is applied it should always be followed up with the protective seal that a good coat of wax provides. Heavy duty plating protection for harsh winter exposure can be obtained by a liberal application of a commercial grade floor wax. This may result in a visible coating not altogether pleasing to the eye, but nonetheless effective as an overlayer.

Armor All "Ultra-Plate" is one product worthy of experimentation. In extreme conditions, Flitz Marine Metal Polish provides protection against corrosion for up to three months per application.

Pride from a competent application can be severely diminished when the admiring eye is drawn to whitish residual deposits in crevices. *The more time spent following up the wax job with detailing, the happier you will be with the product of your effort.*

REMOVING WAX

When discoloration in the wax finish on a Porsche signals a breakdown in its protective shield, it will be necessary to remove or strip away this spent material to secure a new base. The effects of wax must also be voided in preparation for refinishing. Removers, usually found as clear liquid formulas, require application with a clean rag in overlapping strokes. Ditzler DX-330, Prepsol and Acrysol are representative products used professionally for this purpose.

RESTORING SCRATCHES

Abrasions that penetrate only the paint are easiest to remedy, the major requirement being patience. Superficial marks are cured by lightly rubbing the area with a mild (waxless) abrasive to free loose paint. Rinse the blemished area throughly with water to

remove all loose material and compound, then dry. A conservative application of correctly coordinated touch-up paint can be used to fill the cavity. Utilize a brush correspondingly *smaller* than the scratch. Build up thin layers of paint only within the valley till these several applications level with the adjacent paint surface. *Allow several weeks to cure.*

Finish by employing a fine rubbing compound or cutting paste to blend more accurately with surrounding color, sheen and texture. Finalize with wax.

When the metal surface has been scratched, causing the affected area to oxidize, restoration entails more involved preparation. Free the fracture of any remaining loose paint chips, loose dirt and rust with a small knife or similar instrument. Begin the build-up with carefully applied rust-inhibiting paint. When this material dries, fill with a *thin* mixture of body scratch filler paste. Allow a few days and then finish as described earlier. When metal damage is more severe than a scratch, repair may require lead solder and the touch of a skilled professional metal craftsman.

PROPERTIES OF PAINT

Porsche's original factory finish assures many years of good service. When a recent car betrays evidence of having been refinished there is always a reason. Rarely is it one that gives credence to the effort and even more rarely to the structural integrity of the automobile.

In the vintage Porsche original paint becomes an attribute commanding respect and premium value in any market. The quality of original Porsche factory paint as used on 356 and 900 series cars has been acclaimed worldwide. Few considerations in Porsche preservation present more of a dilemma than the problem of when and where to have the car refinished and with what material.

A higher percentage of the manufacturing cost of the Porsche is represented by the paint work than in the production of the U.S. built luxury automobile. The extra DMs have been well spent. As touched upon, aftermarket paint jobs seldom attain the detailing fidelity of the original work. In a rare instance, where costs are no object and certain master craftsmen can be engaged, one may exceed the factory specs. But this is generally a case for the

166

Guinness Book. Not all owners will be in search of a concours-winning finish constructed from thirty coats of meticulously hand-rubbed lacquer, but every owner wants a professional quality effort that does not call attention to itself by its inadequacies.

Preparation is the key to a first class paint job, regardless of material to be used in the finish. All metal reconstruction work and the effort to preserve structural integrity must be of a high order. Ninety percent of the price of a paint job will be reflected from the labor; ten percent from material. It is still possible to get a very respectable paint job for a reasonable round sum when *you* contribute your own finesse in trim removal and detail masking of those fringe areas such as inner panels and suspension components that professional masking might choose to omit. [Illustrated pages 166, 168]

The most effective repainting job is one using exactly the color dictated by the car's original finish. When painted sections usually concealed to the outside, such as the firewall and doorjambs, provide no telltale parting lines the completed effort results in a better quality refinishing.

When a change in color is being considered you will want to weigh the different attributes of light and dark shades. Dark colors *appear cleaner* (when they are clean) and can convey a *depth* which results in a richer luster. By presenting maximum contrast with brightwork they tend to highlight this trim. Contours are enhanced and favorable elements in design seem spotlighted, *provided panel sections are straight and pure*. Cabin temperature, of course, runs several degrees higher in a heat-absorbing dark car during sunny days.

Light colors, being less mirror-like, are less inclined to betray dust and broadcast imperfections in body panels to the casual viewer. They are easier to see in traffic and at night — a distinct safety consideration in a small car. Lighter tones reflect heat and help to keep the interior color. Bright metallic flake finishes require the deft hand of a professional for successful retouching. Experience with silver finishes of established paint formulas would suggest a predictably shorter luster life for this color than for most others.

A working knowledge of paints and their properties, and an acquaintance with preparatory steps will enable you to choose the most effective material for your particular application. Methods

and prices range from the baked synthetic "Any car painted for $39. In by 9, out by 5!" madhouse run through, to the old world craftsmanship of hand-rubbed lacquer in a finish built up of multiple coats. As anyone can see, the preparation time allocated when recoloring a car for $39 would permit little more than a thorough wash. [Illustrated page 170]

Progressive observation of several works in progress at a body shop under consideration can be helpful in determining if capabilities are up to claims. Effective observation requires following the same job or jobs through all stages from the time started, metal prep to the heat lamps and after. Steal with your eyes not only the efforts in reconstruction and refinishing but the order and objectivity exhibited by individual craftsmen as they ply their skills. Look for men working with a surety that translates as style; for men who handle their working tools with mastery but lay them down with gentle respect.You may even detect a kind of overall rhythm or cadence in work underway at the shop that appeals to you.

Basic types of paint material available today include synthethic enamel, acrylic enamel, polyurethane enamel, nitrocellulose lacquer and acrylic lacquer.

Synthetics have been used in car building for some time. Color selection is wide. Few aftermarket shops, however, have ovens capable of duplicating factory drying and curing conditions. Porsche factory colors were applied to the bare body shell *before* rubber, glass and wiring were attached. The drying area in Stuttgart also utilized temperatures higher than those appropriate for fully fitted bodies seeking renovation in the aftermarket. Success with enamel requires dust-free drying time. Acceptable coverage can be rendered through a single coat which requires no rubbing to display a high gloss. Abrasion resistence, once cured, is high. The finish is easy to maintain through regular washing and requires a minimum of polishing. Negative considerations with synthetics involve the problem of tack-free drying and special care for a finished surface that cannot be touched up or spotted-in very effectively with the same material.

Acrylic enamel offers faster drying time. Color selection extends to certain pastel shades that may not be available in the synthetic spectrum. Like the synthetic it covers well with a

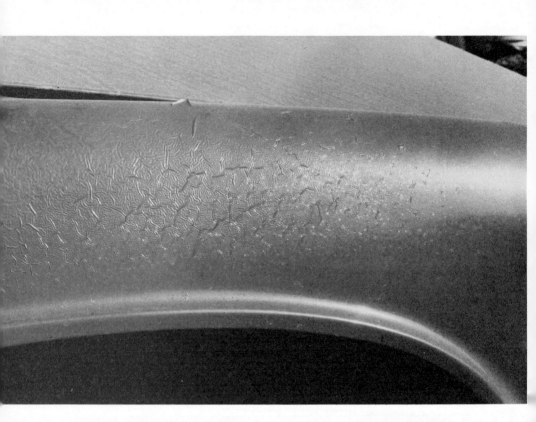

minimum coating. The acrylic is relatively easy to color match and touch up. It provides a forgiving surface for rubbing out soon after application. Porsches have often been refinished with acrylic enamel because it is possible to obtain a final texture and color match that closely approaches the original factory finish.

Urethane finishes adhere admirably to rough surfaces, cover well and bear superior scratch resistance qualities. They are turtle shell tough. Color selection has been focused on the industrial range rather than the commercial, since these products have been principally employed in the aircraft and marine industries. Polyurethane is commonly a two-part paint — pigment and catalyst — resulting in a material suitable for extremely hard conditions, but one in which application is complicated — and more expensive. The average automobile refinishing shop, in the absence of previous experience, probably would not care to become involved with this material for the first time. There is hope on the horizon, for innovations continue and new developments with "monopoxy" materials promise to make tomorrow's task with polyurethane easier.

Nitrocellulose lacquer is ideally compatible with aftermarket procedures. Rapid drying time permits application in small facilities with less than optimum conditions and permits rubbing out only a few hours after spraying. This material goes on flat, polishes well through a hand rubbing stage and can be spotted easily all through its service life. Concours winners claim that subtle color tones and texture can be matched exceedingly well with this material. Meticulous preparation is required. Lacquer does not adhere over certain other paint materials. *Best application is obtained when the body is stripped to bare surface and primed with great care.* Many thin coats are the secret of success. Every minute imperfection in the surface will cause a blemish that is readily detectable because lacquer shrinks into a scratch, transferring the same undulation to the new surface. Special reservations should be taken in the use of primer, for a heavy build-up increases susceptability to chipping in the final lacquer finish.

Acrylic lacquer is similar to nitrocellulose in drying time and hardness of surface. More of the rainbow is available in acrylic materials. Some contend that it may retain a shine longer and actually outlast nitrocellulose on the calendar. Some experts contend, however, that while the long life properties may be present, acrylic lacquer cannot provide the intensity of light refraction so appreciated by advocates of the traditional mirror-like nitrocellulose material.

Enamel, being more flexible when dry than lacquer, is less prone to crack. Enamel is the best way to go whenever the car features any notable aluminum construction because of its ability to ride altered surfaces, by expanding and contracting to conform to the changes that prevail during the service life of panels of such soft material. Traditional preference among restorers is for the nitrocellulose lacquers, in spite of an established tendency to crack with maturation. The majority of every-day-use Porsches seem to wind up being refinished in acrylic enamel.

As each paint material embodies distinctive positive and negative values, the shop you engage should be consulted for specific maintenance recommendations based on an analysis of the material presently covering your Porsche.

PLATING COMPOUNDS

Recent developments in chemistry have brought a new product to the automobile finish preservative field. Many dealers have elected to apply this "miracle" compound — an acrylic exterior protectant — to new Porsches on the sales floor. Representative is "Perma-Plate" produced by Siskin Enterprises which promotes a Du Pont Teflon content. The material produces a hard shell finish that outlasts wax and claims even to resist corrosive salt air and gasoline. Periodic application of a special "renewer" containing petroleum distillates is required for maintenance. A follow-up supply is generally furnished with the treated automobile at time of delivery.

Although this protectant is regarded as a servicable "extra" by some Porsche owners, a few have filed complaints of poor or negligent initial application. A limited, non-transferable three-year warranty on new car applications and a similar one-year warranty on used cars is offered by the maker. The warranty is predicated on proper application and maintenance.

Professional charges for this treatment have been noted in the $200 range. Comparable "poly-sealants" with generic designations can be purchased by the do-it-yourself owner for a fraction. Several established preservative product companies, including Blue Coral and Starshine Group, offer compounds in this category.

CARE OF RUBBER PARTS

While rubber is adversely affected by petroleum derivatives, extremes of temperature and ozone, and is subject to dimensional instability, hardening and downright rot, its special properties make the material ideal for a host of applications in automobile construction. [Illustrated page 174]

As rubber parts deteriorate, their original purposes are no longer well served. Bumper strips contract and break away; seal strips permit wind, dust and rain to enter and create air noise and rattles. Deterioration of materials adjacent to the rubber follows. Prolonging the useful life of these resilient components requires a consistent effort, as well as appreciation of what rubber is and what it is not. It is an excellent buffer material for joining like and unlike materials; it is never used as a structural member.

Repeated applications of talcum powder on rubber insulation will extend original qualities. Silicone spray used to ease window opening and closing will lubricate and preserve window channels. The liquid product called Armor All, which prevents cracking by restoring a measure of moisture in dead dry surfaces, can be used both to preserve and enhance appearance of upholstery and trim, window seals, instrument panels, tirewalls and perhaps most significantly, tired weatherstripping. Rubber parts should be cleaned with rubber cement thinner before treating. Working with intact seals, a treatment with Armor All every six months should extend useful life substantially.

Weatherstripping that has become dislocated but remains pliable and complete can be reset with weatherstrip adhesive made for this purpose, or with rubber or trim cement. Both surfaces should be cleaned with thinner before reaffixing. When refitting, an inspection should first be made to determine the desired effect. Chances are the weatherstrip was originally molded with this particular location dictating its configuration. When possible, apply first the center section or the area where the most critical lineup is required, then work out toward the ends. Stretching at any point may result in the strip failing to fulfill its primary purpose.

Rotted or incomplete weatherstrip necessitates replacement. There is reassurance in the fact that *the cash value of your Porsche will rise to at least cover the cost of the replacement parts when these rubber sections are properly renewed.*

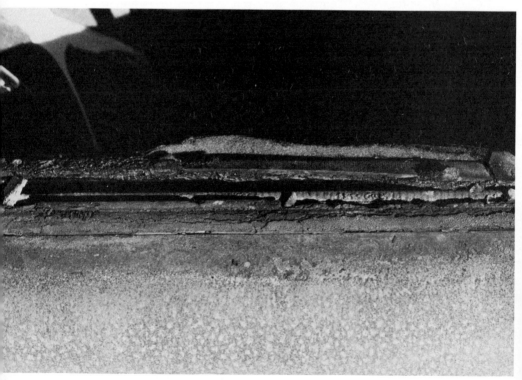

What can destroy the interior of a Porsche as surely as that eight inch screwdriver projecting from the hip pocket of a careless mechanic? Little can be more discouraging to the prideful owner than to be confronted by surprise with the adverse results of water leaking.

Unfortunately, locating the precise point of seepage may be difficult. Particularly among older window and door seals, water can enter through a small fracture at one point and flow along inside — concealed by trim — to a remote spot, before evidencing itself as a stain, drip or puddle. If a detailed inspection of the subject exterior fails to betray the point of penetration it may be necessary to strip the suspected interior area of trim and carpet in order to find it.

Station yourself inside. Enlist a confederate to slowly spray the car to simulate rain and traffic splashes while you scrutinize the bare ribbed inner body and spot the place where weatherproofing has failed. The most effective hosing follows a directional pattern, like across the bottom, up one side and down,across the top, the other side, up and down, etc.

When the condition of weatherstripping around the doors of a pre-1974 Porsche warrants replacement, the opportunity is presented to upgrade the car from original specs. Advances in rubber technology have resulted in a product with closer tolerances and more sophisticated construction. Therefore, your carefully rendered replacement effort may result in door seals at least as good as they were originally.

The owner of an open Porsche soon begins unconsciously to inspect his top fabric for cracks, tears or holes on a regular basis. Visual examination of hinge plates and drip moldings should be included.

Necessary resealing should be carried out before any interior restoration is attempted. Waterproofing as soon as a leak is discovered will prevent later disappointment, as well as the necessity for more elaborate corrective measures. *Sealing leaks is the initial step toward effective care of the interior.*

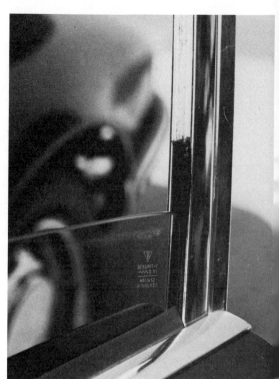

INTERIOR CLEANING AND PRESERVATION

The owner who holds his car to concours standards knows from experience that the most efficient approach to interior cleaning is to remove all detachable components so each piece can be detailed separately with full access — the seats independently of the carpets, etc.

The larger debris revealed when carpets have been removed can be whisked out. This should be followed by a thorough vacuuming. Several efficient, hand-held compact models are now offered, including one from Black & Decker. One of these might find a spot in the compartment with your tools.

Volatile cleaning agents should be avoided in the interior of your Porsche. Solvents such as gasoline, thinner and turpentine are not suitable for use anywhere on a fine car, let alone the interior. Consideration of laundry soaps and caustic cleansers should also be dismissed. Just about every soiled element in your cockpit will respond surprisingly well, and safely, to a mild castile soap used with warm water.

Leather

Supple leather hide is universally accepted as the most luxurious and naturally functional material for seating and interior trim. If your Porsche is finished in real leather protect it by regular washing *before* dirt builds up noticably in the creases, using a mild, non-detergent soap. Follow up with light buffing to dry and attain that subtle glow. *Leather should never be touched by an abrasive cleaner.*

Genuine leather trim always requires special care, with neglect quickly evident. Leaving leather exposed to the hot sun can boil out its softness quickly. Keeping real hide clean and avoiding sun and heat exposure as much as possible will prolong life for those properties most appreciated.

In addition to cleaning, cowhide must be "fed" periodically, perhaps twice a year. This entails coating outer surfaces with Hide Food, Lexol or Clausen's Rejuvenator Oil. Saddle soap is not recommended. While actually doing little to renew leather it often leaves behind dirt-catching residue of its own. When leather is pleated, cleaning must reach deep into every seam to discourage concealed dirt from rotting the stitching. The Clausen company

also makes a crack-filling compound for aged leather that may, when used in conjunction with recoloring, cosmetically for utility purposes postpone the need for reupholstering.

Vinyl

A significant difference between natural leather and synthetic vinyl "leather" is that oils cannot be replenished in the manufactured product. Another related contrast is in porosity: while leather breathes, vinyl does not.

Knowledgeable trim people claim that vinyl looks its best when cleaned with plain soap and water. There is something to be said for this. Lexol, Armor All, or any wax or silicone application on vinyl produces an *uncharacteristic gloss* not inherent in the original finish. Over-restoration is never desirable because it calls undue attention to itself. Meguiar's line now offers a two-stage preservation product similar to Armor All but compounded especially for vinyl so that it does not leave the flashy synthetic sheen of others.

Once vinyl is fed with a surface preservative, the demand for reapplication will be frequent; its non-absorbent composition permits only a coating to lie atop the material. Vinyl is dramatically affected by ultraviolets, ozone and general light; it is destroyed by excessive heat. [Illustrated page 178] These products do little to protect against the sun's rays but may keep the surface free from other impurities that may lead to deterioration.

The most effective measure for preserving vinyl indefinitely is to shelter it from any prolonged direct exposure to the sun. Vinyl reacts well to a soft detergent for cleaning, with strong mixtures invariably leaving a whitish film. A mild soap, soft brush and terry cloth towel work best.

One of the very few disturbing aspects of older Porsche 900 series ownership is the practically certain mortality affecting the dash top. [Illustrated page 180] *Minor cracking induced by tight fit apparently comes to the central area regardless of the care exercised.* Unfortunately, these fractures cannot be effectively repaired and obscured. Many attempts have been made with varying degrees of artistry to fill that little crack between the speaker grille and the vent slot with some miraculous black compound that might magically cause it to disappear. All have failed. Replacement of the dash top is necessary.

179

New replacements are stocked by dealerships. Simply securing a new section and bringing it home to "drop in" will not be the end of it. Reports confirm that these dash pieces generally do not provide a ready fit. Tolerances are practically non-existent, a factor that has caused many an owner effort at installation to develop into a nightmare of wrestling with a buckling form.

Nonetheless, if you are considering this independent effort, be apprised that it requires removal of the windshield as well as other parts. *Dash top replacement is better relegated to an authorized dealer where a craftsman who has done it before will be assigned to perform your job.*

Fabrics

The fabric interior can be a beauty to behold, but only when it is literally tight, full-colored and spotless. Since most materials used in automobile trim are subject to stretching, are color fugitive and are easily stained, the fabric interior is the most difficult to maintain and renovate.

Sustained exposure to the beating sun is probably the prime cause of stretching, fading and deterioration of both stitching and fabric. Preservation is a matter of avoiding this exposure.

Staining may be less avoidable. Before attempting any chemical treatment, pick up as much of the offending residue as possible with the tacky side of masking tape, or even a big brother product like duct tape. Was it a water leak that caused the stain? Or was it coffee, chocolate, ice cream, or? The first step requires knowing what substance caused the stain. Only then can the proper chaser be introduced in an effort to diminish the mark. Your Owner's Manual may recommend procedures for cleaning some of the more common stains on specific Porsche fabrics.

When employing a commercial cleaning fluid on a fabric stain, first test the material on an obscure area to assure compatability. After confirmation, dampen a clean cloth with the fluid and lightly rub the perimeter of the spot with strokes toward its center. Change to a new part of the cloth almost continuously as you gradually reduce the spot inward. The object of all this care will be to remove not only the spot but also to diminish its telltale ring.

Common products, such as Scotchgard and Thermo-Guard, effectively seal upholstery against common spills and stains with an impervious coating, while claiming to improve tensile strength and abrasion resistance without altering texture.

The Headlining

Though the headliner is potentially the largest single contributing piece in retaining cabin odors some owners are reportedly so accustomed to unmaintained headlining that they assume the dull yellows and grays to be factory-issued tints. These discolorations result from smoking and from collecting dirt and impurities from the outer atmosphere by driving or parking with the windows open.

Any improvement in appearance by cleaning can come only from an even, consistent and meticulous brushing or scrubbing. Experiment sparingly with a flat scrubbing sponge or brush, using the same soap you use for the rest of the interior. The cleaning instrument should be rinsed continuously. Work up from the sides toward the center to "lift" foreign particles up and out of the fabric. Once the results of your efforts begin to show a welcome contrast with the remaining lining, you will be encouraged to complete the job even though the inverted scrubbing position — working against gravity — is necessarily awkward and tedious.

A clean headliner is among the most efficient interior deodorizers.

Carpeting

Porsche carpets should be subject to the same preservative treatment accorded those in your home, unless specified otherwise. Dirt lodged in the nap, acting as a grinding compound, is the common villain. Except during spot touch-up cleaning, carpets should always be removed and laid flat out of the sun. By vacuuming, then shampooing and then vacuuming again, you can bring all but the severely worn piece back to a near original state.

For difficult stains and spots, apply mild soapsuds with a sponge and wipe off with a clean sponge. Allow to dry and brush thoroughly with a whisk broom. A tablespoon of ammonia in the suds may help to refresh a faded color. The results of re-dying or spray-painting Porsche carpets can be conspiciously self-evident, not alone in appearance but also in the telltale odor the process introduces to the cabin.

182

Coco mats and sisal carpets are acceptable extras to enhance an interior. They do a superior job of protecting the original carpets in a Porsche, new or vintage, while also providing additional sound deadening.

In wet weather it is advisable to "slip cover" the carpets with a coverall prepared from ducking or canvas tenting which can be kept rolled and ready in the trunk. In a pinch, towels or even newspapers can be spread to collect the bulk of mud and absorb stray water that may be introduced by wet footwear.

The concours owner carries the protective cover idea farther, masking off carpets, as well as upholstery and trim panels, before going in to his mechanic for service.

Seating

Estimates cite that the driver's seat receives up to fifty times the wear of the companion seat. After a few years in service, particularly when the driver is inclined toward Levi jeans or other clothing with a tough surface, crown and stress points in the seat upholstery begin to reveal a pattern from fair wear and tear. In older cars the left and right seats can be interchanged. The owner may switch seats and in effect balance out the wear, provided it is not already too prominently advanced.

As the seats feature seatback reclining levers in opposite positions, it is necessary to relocate these parts. Remove the seat assemblies and their respective sliding rails. Switch rail assemblies and reinstall. Exchange the positions of the floor rails. Then bring in the seats left-for-right and the locations of controls will be as before.

The seat cover should never be introduced in a Porsche to conceal faults in the original upholstery. Certain covers offered for the car represent useful additions only when worn as coveralls over a good suit underneath. With a new car, it is often suggested that the owner enjoy the full effect of his vehicle's original upholstery for an initial period. Later, when the novelty of newness begins to recede, he may opt for sheepskin covers or an equivalent and wisely have something different to enjoy.

All measures taken to preserve the pristine originality of upholstery and trim are strides toward stabilizing intrinsic value at the apex of the curve.

Bright Trim

It would be an irreversible error to attempt to restore interior brightwork with so-called chrome polish, in reality a mild rubbing compound. This material would do much to "bring back" the bumper or bullet-shaped "Dagmar" overriders on the front of a 1955 Cadillac. But the garnish in the cockpit of a Porsche is not steel-backed hard chromium plating but soft aluminum and plastic shrouded in chrome-like finish.

Use of a dampened cloth or sponge and working as dry as the extent of dirt permits will leave the trim unmarred. Introduce water sparingly so that it performs only the job desired. No excess should be permitted to work in behind the trim panels. With fiberboard backing these panels are subject to permanent warp if subjected to heavy moisture. If you choose to wax this brightwork, determine first that the product you apply is not a *polish* wax containing abrasives.

Engine & Compartment

Porsche owners are more likely than many other motorists to demonstrate their concern for overall performance by carrying on their cosmetic maintenance inside the motor compartment. A thorough cleaning of the engine, accessories and surrounding space once or twice a year, not only reflects pride in the whole automobile but reduces the hazard from those accumulated combustibles that eventually glaze over the unattended internal combustion engine.

After the first complete engine degreasing, ensuing cleaning jobs will be more in the form of maintenance. The engine should be warm when the job is approached, the better to dislodge and dissolve exterior deposits. Contemporary degreasers and carburetor cleaners make this dirty job relatively simple. "Gunk" is a traditional favorite.

Accessories such as the air filter housing should be removed. Carburetor throats must be effectively plugged and hose and electrical connections should be masked off with tape. After coding for replacement, remove the spark plug cables and cover the distributor with a plastic bag.

Using a dull knife or flatblade screwdriver, scrape off as much of the grease and oil deposits as possible. Liberally apply the degreaser selected, observing any particular directions offered and let the material work for about half an hour. After soaking, wipe away the grease and dirt that has been broken down, using a dry rag. Follow with a strong stream of water from a garden hose to clear the surfaces. Use soap and water for a final cleaning. Rinse till all treated castings and assemblies gleam as though the engine had been freshly assembled.

Focus now on the carburetors and apply a special cleaner if it seems necessary. Products offered for this purpose are generally quite effective. "Gumout" spray is representative of the field. A toothbrush makes an effective tool. Light application of steel wool to residual matter may also be required.

Thoroughly dry the entire compartment with rags. An air hose could be used at this point for final drying. Relocate any assemblies that were removed and restore disengaged links and wires. *The degreasing agent will have removed the lubrication from the carburetor linkage. It is critical that such action points be relubed immediately before running to prevent the obvious possibility of a sticking throttle.*

Start the car. Go for a short drive to determine that everything is functioning properly. This run will also dry off any excess and trapped water. Paint touch up that may be required in the engine compartment can be done best at this time. Careful masking is a prerequisite.

If a warning light should go on unexpectedly within 48 hours after such an extensive cleaning, it may generally be traced to a loose or separated connection. First look to the generator failure warning light connections, then to others. Diagrams in your Porsche Owner's Manual will reveal the location of the terminal that corresponds to each light.

The engine can be kept up by periodic wiping with cleanser. Regular inspection of the fuel line is recommended, this being the usual source of any fire. Assure that no kinks restrict the flow. Replace at first signs of deterioration.

A retrospective moment in Ferry Porsche's autobiography presents a worthy challenge.

"My father had always retained an intense interest in British locomotives. The war had not affected that. He had always been impressed with the shine and polish of these engines and the meticulous way in which they were maintained so that they managed to look new regardless of their age."

A Numerical Guide to Series, Specifications and Vintage

Year of Mfg.	Model & Engine Designation	HP DIN @RPM	Engine Ser. Nos.	Chassis Serial Numbers Coupe	Chassis Serial Numbers Convertible
1950	356/1100	40@4200	0101–0411	5001–5410	
1951	356/1100	40@4200	0412–0099	5132–5162	
			10001–10137	5411–5600	
			1001–1099	10001–10170	
	356/1300	44@4200	20001–20821	10350–10432	
	From Oct 356/1500	60@5000	30001–30737	10531–11125	
1952	356/1100	40@4200	10138–10151		10433–10469
	356/1300	44@4200	20822–21297	11126–12084	
	Till Sept 356/1500	60@5000	30738–30750		12301–12387
	From Sept 356/1500	55@4400	30751–31025	50001–50098	
	From Oct 356/1500S	70@5000	40001–40117		15001–15116
1953	356/1100	40@4200	10152–10161		
	356/1300	44@4200	21298–21636		
	356/1500	55@4400	31026–32569	50099–51645	60001–60394
	356/1500S	70@5000	40118–40685		
	From Nov 356/1300S	60@5500	50001–50017		
1954	356/1100	40@4200	10162–10199		
	356/1300	44@4200	21637–21780		
	Till May 356/1300S	60@5500	50018–50099		
	June to Nov 356/1300S	44@4200	21781–21999		
	Till Nov 356/1500	55@4400	32570–33899	51646–53008	60395–60722
	Till Nov 356/1500S	70@5000	40686–40999		
	356/1300	44@4200	22001–22021		
	356/1300S	60@5500	50101–		
	From Nov 356/1500	55@4400	33901–34119		
	356/1500S	70@5000	41001–41048		
1955	356/1300	44@4200	22022–22245		
	Till Oct 356/1300S	60@5500	–50127		
	356/1500	55@4400	34120–35790	53009–55000	60723–81900
	356/1500S	70@5000	41049–41999		
(1956 Model)	From Oct 356A/1300	44@4200	22246–22273		
	356A/1300S	60@5500	50128–50135		
	356A/1600	60@4500	60001–60608		
	356A/1600S	75@5000	80001–80110	55001–55390	61001–61069
1956	356A/1300	44@4200	22274–22471		
	356A/1300S	60@5500	50136–50155		
	356A/1600	60@4500	60609–63926	55391–58311	61070–61499
	356A/1600S	75@5000	80111–80756		
1957	Till Sept 356A/1300	44@4200	22472–22999	58312–59090	61500–61700
	356A/1300S	60@5500	50156–50999	From March	
	356A/1600	60@4500	63927–66999	100001–101692	61701–61892
	356A/1600S	75@5000	80757–81199		
	From Sept 356A/1600	60@4500	67001–68216	(T 2)	
	356A/1600S	75@5000	81201–81521	101693–102504	150001–150149
1958	356A/1600	60@4500	68217–72468	102505–106174	150150–151531
	356A/1600S	75@5000	81522–83145		
1959	Till Sept 356A/1600	60@4500	72469–79999	106175–108917	151532–152475
	356A/1600S	75@5000	83146–84770		
(1960 Model)	From Sept 356B/1600	60@4500	600101–601500		
	356B/1600S	75@5000	84771–85550	(T 5) 108918–110237	152476–152943
1960	356B/1600	60@4500	601501–604700		
	356B/1600S	75@5000	85551–88320	110238–114650	152944–154560
	356B/1600S-90	90@5500	800101–802000		
1961	356B/1600	60@4500	604701–606799	114651–117476	
	Till Sept 356B/1600S	75@5000	88321–89999		
			085001–085670	Karm./Hardt. 200001–201048	154561–155569
	356B/1600S-90	90@5500	802001–803999		

Year of Mfg.	Model & Engine Designation	HP DIN @RPM	Engine Ser. Nos.	Chassis Serial Numbers Coupe	Convertible
	(1962 Model)			(T 6)	
	From Sept 356B/1600	60@4500	606801–607760	117601–118950	
	356B/1600S	75@5000	700001–701200	Karm./Hardt.	155601–156200
	356B/1600S-90	90@5500	804001–804630	201601–202200	
1962	Till July 356B/1600	60@4500	607751–608900	118951–121099	
	356B/1600S	75@5000	701201–702800	Karm./Hardt.	
	356B/1600S-90	90@5500	804631–805600	202201–202299	156201–156999
				Karm./Coupe	
				210001–210899	
	(1963 Model)			(T 6) (abroad)	
	From July 356B/1600	60@4500	608901–610000	121100–123042	
	356B/1600S	75@5000	702801–705050	Karm./Coupe	157000–157768
	356B/1600S-90	90@5500	805601–806600	210900–212171	
1963	Till July 356B/1600	60@4500	610001–611000		
			0600501–0600600		
			611001–611200		
	356B/1600S	75@5000	705051–706000	125239–132304	157769–158700
			0700501–0701200	Karm./Coupe	
			706001–707200	212172–214400	
	356B/1600S-90	90@5500	806601–807000		
			0800501–0801000		
			807001–807400		
	(1964 Model)				
	From July 356C/1600C	75@5200	710001–711870	126001–128104	159001–159832
			730001–731102	Karm./Coupe	
	356C/1600SC	95@5800	810001–811001	215001–216738	
			820001–820522		
	From Sept 911	130@6100	711871–716804	300001–300235	
	356C/1600C	75@5200	731103–733027	128105–131927	
					159833–161577
	356C/1600SC	95@5800	811002–813562	216739–221482	
			820523–821701		

Model Year	Model & Engine Designation	HP DIN @RPM	Engine Ser. Nos.	Chassis Serial Numbers Coupe	Convertible
1965	356C/1600C	75@5200	716805 etc.	138928 etc.	161578 etc.
			733028 etc.	Karm./Coupe	
	356C/1600SC	95@5800	813563 etc.	221483 etc.	
			821702 etc.		
	911	130@6100	900361–903550	300236–303390	
	912	90@5800	740001–744210	350001–351970	
			830001–832090		
1966	911	130@6100	903551	303391–305100	
			907000		
	911	130@6100	907001		
			909000		
	912	90@5800	E744211	351971–353000	
			750001	454470–485100	
			I832091		
			836000		
1967	911	130@6100	909001	305101–307350	
			911000		
	911	130@6100	911001		
			911190		
			960001		
	911S	160@6600	961144	305101S–307360S	
			E750001	354001–354970	
	912	90@5800	753430	458101–461140	
			I836001		
			836610		
	911	130@6100	911191	307351–308522	
			912050	307361S–308523S	
			961141	354971–355601	
	911S	160@6600	962178	461141–463204	
	912	90@5800	E753431	500001–500718	
			756195	500001S–500718S	
			I836611	550001–550544	
			837070		

Model Year	Model & Engine Designation	HP DIN @RPM	Engine Ser. Nos.	Chassis Serial Numbers Coupe	Convertible
1968	911USA	130@6100	3280001	11835001–11830001–11880001	
	911USA	130@6100	3380001		
	911L	130@6100	3080001	11810001–11860001	
	911L	130@6100	3180001		
	911T	110@5800	2080001	11825001–11820001–11870001	
	911T	110@5800	2180001		
	911S	160@6600	4080001	11800001–11850001	
	911S	160@6600	4180001		
	911LUSA	130@6100	3280001	11805001–11855001	
	911LUSA	130@6100	3380001		
	912	90@5800	I1080001	12800001–12820001–12870001	
			E1085001		
	912USA	90@5800	1280001		
1969	912	90@5800	4090001–4091499	129000001–129009999	
	912	90@5800	4091501–4092999	129010001–129019999	
	912	90@5800	4093001–4099999	129020001–129029999	
	911T	110@5800	6190001–6192999	119100001–119109999	
	911T	110@5800	6193001–6194999	119110001–119119999	
	911T	110@5800	6195001–6197999	119120001–119129999	
	911E	140@6500	6198001–6199999	119200001–119209999	
	911E	140@6500	6290001–6297999	119210001–119219999	
	911E	140@6500	6298001–6299999	119220001–119229999	
	911S	170@6800	6390001–6399999	119300001–119309999	
	911S	170@6800		119310001–119319999	
1970	911T	125@5800	6100001–6102999	9110100001–9110109999	
	911T	125@5800	6103001–6104999	9110110001–9110119999	
	911T	125@5800	6105001–6107999	9110120001–9110129999	
	911E	155@6200	6108001–6109999	9110200001–9110209999	
	911E	155@6200	6200001–6207999	9110210001–9110219999	
	911E	155@6200	6208001–6209999	9110220001–9110229999	
	911S	180@6500	6300001–6309999	9110300001–9110309999	
	911S	180@6500		9110310001–9110319999	
	914/6	110@5800	6400001–6403000		
	914/6	110@5800	6403001–6404000	9140430001–9140439999	
	914/6	110@5800	6404001–6407000		
	914/6	110@5800	6407001–6408000		
	914	80@4900	WO 000001– WO 057460	4702900001–4702913312	
1971	911T	125@5800	6210001–6218000	9111100001–9111102583	
	911T	125@5800	6310001–6318000	9111110001–9111113476	
	911T	125@5800	6110001–6114000	9111120001–9111121934	
	911E	155@6200	6218001–6219999	9111200001–9111201088	
	911E	155@6200	6119001–6119500	9111210001–9111210935	
	911S	180@6500	6114001–6119000	9111300001–9111301430	
	911S	180@6500	6115001–6119999	9111310001–9111310788	
	911S	180@6500	6318001–6318500		
	914/6	110@5800	6410001–6413000		
	914/6	110@5800	6413001–6414000	9141430001–9144530443	
	914/6	110@5800	6414001–6417000		
	914/6	110@5800	6417001–6418000		
	914	80@4900	WO 057461– WO 129581	4712900001–4712916231	
1972		SAE Net @RPM			
	911T	133@5600	6120001–6124478	9112100001–9112102931	
	911T	133@5600	6129001–6129293	9112110001–9112111821	
	911E	157@6200	6220001–6221765	9112200001–9112201124	
	911E	157@6200	6229001–6229248	9112210001–9112210861	
	911S	181@6500	6320001–6322586	9112300001–9112301750	
	911S	181@6500	6329001–6329147	9112310001–9112310989	
	914	76@4900	WO129582– EA057000	4722901400–4722921580	
1973	911T	134@5700	6130021-6131926	9113100011-9113101261	
	911T	134@5700	6139021-6139149	9113110011-9113110801	
	911E	157@6200	6133021-6136092	9113101501-9113103444	
	911E	157@6200	6139321-6139502	9113111001-9113112302	
	911S	181@6500	6230021-6232125	9113200011-9113201366	
	911S	181@6500	6239021-6239319	9113210011-9113211055	
	911		6330021-6332231	9113300011-9113301430	
	Carrera RS	200@6300	6339021-6339136	9113310011-9113310925	
	914 1.7	76@4900	EA0057001–96608		
	914 1.7			4732900001-4732927660	
	California	69@5000	EB0000001– 09703		
	914 2.0	91@4900	GA0000001– 06765		

*ST = Standard Transmission   AT = Automatic   T = Targa
SP = Sportomatic   **C = Coupe

Model Year	Model and Engine Designation	HP SAE Net @ RPM	Engine Serial Numbers*	Chassis Serial Numbers**
1974	911	143 @ 5700	ST 6140001-6146625 SP 6149001-6149517	C 9114100001-9114104014 T 9114110001-9114113110
	911S	167 @ 5800	ST 6340001-6342804 SP 6349001-6349236	C 9114300001-9114301359 T 9114310001-9114310898
	Carrera	167 @ 5800	ST 6340001-6342804 SP 6349001-6349236	C 9114400001-9114400528 T 9114410001-9114410246
	914 1.8 914 2.0	72 @ 4800 91 @ 4900	EC 0000001-EC 0037551 GA 0006766-GA 0015021	C 47290001-4742921370 C 47290001-4742921370
1975	911S	157 @ 5800	ST 6450001-6452440 SP 6459001-6459135	C 9115200001-9115202310 T 9115210001-9115211517
	911S (Cal.)	152 @ 5800	ST 6550001-6551783 SP 6559001-6559082	C 9115200001-9115202310 T 9115210001-9115211517
	Carrera	157 @ 5800	ST 6450001-6452440 SP 6459001-6459135	C 9115400001-9115400395 T 9115410001-9115410174
	Carrera (Cal.)	152 @ 5800	ST 6550001-6551783 SP 6559001-6559082	C 9115400001-9115400395 T 9115410001-9115410174
	914 1.8 914 2.0	72 @ 4900 84 @ 4900	EC 0037552-EC 0045072 EG 0000001-GC 0002914	C 4752900001-4752911368 C 4752900001-4752911368
1976	911S	157 @ 5800	ST 6460021-6462305 SP 6569021-6569160	C 9116200001-9116202079 T 9116210001-9116212175
	911S (Cal.)	157 @ 5800	ST 6560021-6561832 SP 6569021-6569160	C 9116200001-9116202079 T 9116210001-9116212175
	912E	86 @ 4900	ST 4060021-4062115	C 9126000001-9126002099
	Turbo Carrera	234 @ 5500	ST 6860021-6860541	C 9306800001-9306800530
	914 2.0	84 @ 4900	GC 0002915-GC 0006946	C 4762900001-4762904100
1977	924	95 @ 5500 110 @ 5750	XH 000021-XH 0007201 XG 300021-XG 0302872	C 9247200001-9247235789 C 9247200001-9247235789
	924 (Cal.)	95 @ 5500 110 @ 5750	XF 000001- XE 100050-	C 9247200001-9247235789 C 9247200001-9247235789
	911S	157 @ 5800	ST 6270021-6276041 SP 6279021-6279113	C 9117200001-9117203381 T 9117210001-9117212747
	911S (Cal.)	157 @ 5800	ST 6560001-	C 9117200001-9117203381
	Turbo Carrera	234 @ 5500	ST 6870021-6870737	C 9307800001-9307800727
1978	924	110 @ 5750	XG 0302811-XG 309486	C 9248200001-9248211638
	924 (Cal.)	110 @ 5750	XE 000001-XE 108453	C 9248200001-9248211638
	911SC	172 @ 5500	ST 6280021-6282800	C 9118200001-9118202436 T 9118210001-9118212579
	911SC (Cal.)	172 @ 5500	ST 6580001-6582241	C 9118200001-9118202436 T 9118210001-9118212579
	928	219 @ 5250	ST 8280021-8281063 AT 8289021-8289187	C 9288200001-9288201139 C 9288200001-9288201139
	Turbo	253 @ 5430	ST 6880021-6880305	C 9308800001-9308800461
	Turbo (Cal.)	253 @ 5430	ST 6881001-6881187	C 9308800001-9308800461
1979	924 924	110 @ 5750	ST XG 309492-XG 314737 AT XG 109074-XG 314983	C 9249200001-9249209636 C 9249200001-9249209636
	924 (Cal.) 924 (Cal.)	110 @ 5750 110 @ 5750	ST XE 108846-XE 110720 AT XE 109061-XE 113033	C 9249200001-9249209636 C 9249200001-9249209636
	911SC	172 @ 5500	ST 6290001-6291358	C 9119200001-9119202013 T 9119210001-9119211965
	911SC (Cal.)	172 @ 5500	ST 6590001-6591646	C 9119200001-9119202013 T 9119210001-9119211965
	928	219 @ 5250	ST 8290001-8291716 AT 8295001-8295710	C 9289200001-9289202285 C 9289200001-9289202285
	Turbo	261 @ 5500	ST 6890001-6890850	C 9309800001-9309801200
	Turbo (Cal.)	261 @ 5500	ST 6891001-6891374	C 9309800001-9309801200
1980	924 924 924 Turbo 911SC 928 928	110 @ 5750 110 @ 5750 143 @ 5500 172 @ 5500 220 @ 5500 220 @ 5500	UC 000001 UC 000000 31020001 ST 6400001 ST 8100001 AT 8105001	C 92A0430001- C 92A0430001- C 93A0150001- C 91A0140001- C 92A0810001- C 92A0810001-

BIBLIOGRAPHY

Aaltonen, Rauno, *Revolution am Steur – Die Neue Fahrtechnik,* Munich 1979.

Boschen, Lothar and Barth, Jurgen, *The Porsche Book,* New York, 1977.

Boyce, Terry, *Car Interior Restoration,* Blue Ridge Summit (PA), 1975.

Brickell, David and Cole, Lee S., *Vehicle Theft Investigation,* Santa Cruz (CA), 1975.

Campbell, Colin, *The Sports Car – Its Design and Performance,* London, 1969.

Cotton, Michael, *The Porsche 911 and Derivatives/A Collector's Guide,* London, 1980.

Frère, Paul, *Porsche 911 Story,* New York, 1976.

Loosbrock, John F., *The Safe Driving Handbook,* New York, 1970.

Ludvigsen, Karl, *Porsche – Excellence Was Expected,* Princeton (NJ), 1977.

Moriarty, Michael G., *Porsche Now and Then,* Waterbury (CT), 1974.

Porsche, Ferry, *We at Porsche,* Garden City, 1976.

Post, Dan R., *Volkswagen, Nine Lives Later,* Arcadia (CA), 1966

Sleightholme, J.D., *Fitting Out,* New York, 1963.

Sloniger, Jerry, *Porsche 911 Guide,* New York, 1976.

Sponsel, Heinz, *Porsche-Autos-Weltrekorde,* Hannover (West Germany), 1953.

Till, Anthony, *What You Should Know Before You Buy a Car,* Los Angeles, 1968.

Webster, William H., *Crime in the United States 1978,* Washington, D.C., 1978.

Widger, Bill, *How to Get 200,000 Miles Out of Your Car,* New York, 1975.

Zadig, Ernest A., *The Boatman's Guide to Modern Marine Materials,* New York, 1974.

Principal Periodicals:

Automobile Quarterly, Car and Driver, Christophorus, FBI Law Enforcement Bulletin, Forbes, Gmund, Money, Motor Sport, Motor Trend, Road & Track, Porsche Panorama, Porsche Owners Club Newsletter, Safer Motoring, Skinned Knuckles, Sports Car Graphic, Sports Car Illustrated, TIME, U.S. News & World Report, VW & Porsche

Newspapers:

Los Angeles Times, Wall Street Journal

INDEX